Coronations Past, Present and Future

Essays
by
Henry Everett
Paul Bradshaw
Colin Buchanan

Edited by
Paul Bradshaw

THE ALCUIN CLUB and the GROUP FOR RENEWAL OF WORSHIP (GROW)
The Alcuin Club, which exists to promote the study of Christian liturgy in general and of Anglican liturgy in particular, traditionally published a single volume annually for its members. This ceased in 1986 but resumed in 1992. Similarly, GROW was responsible from 1975 to 1986 for the quarterly 'Grove Liturgical Studies'. Since the beginning of 1987 the two have sponsored a Joint Editorial Board to produce 'Joint Liturgical Studies', of which the present Study is no. 38. There are lists on pages 45-46 in this Study, and further details are available from the address below. Both also produce separate publications.

THE COVER PICTURE
is a design by Lyn Stone

ACKNOWLEDGMENTS
The illustrations on pages 20 and 21 below are reproduced by kind permission of the Dean and Chapter of Westminster.

First Impression September 1997
ISSN 0951-2667
ISBN 1 85174 355 3

GROVE BOOKS LIMITED
RIDLEY HALL RD   CAMBRIDGE   CB3 9HU

CONTENTS

CHAPTER   PAGE

Introduction by The Editor, Paul Bradshaw   5

1. The English Coronation Rite: From the Middle Ages to the Stuarts:
   by Henry Everett   7
   Illustrations of the Coronation of James II appended to chapter 1
   Ground-plan of the Abbey   20
   Perspective looking West   21

2. Coronations from the Eighteenth to the Twentieth Centuries:
   by Paul Bradshaw   22
   Diagrammatic Outline of Structure of the Coronation Rite of 1953   .   .   . 32

3. The Next Coronation
   by Colin Buchanan   34

THE CONTRIBUTORS

Henry Everett is Priest-in-Charge of All Saints, Downshire Square, Reading; his essay, entitled 'TheEnglish Coronation Rite of 1685: A Study in Liturgy and Politics' won the Gregory Dix Memorial Award for a study of a liturgical text in 1995; his M.Phil. dissertation was on the sacramental theology of kingship.

Paul Bradshaw is Professor of Liturgy, University of Notre Dame, Indiana, USA, erstwhile of the Church of England Liturgical Commission and currently resident and teaching in England whilst on the faculty of Notre Dame University. He is the Editor of this Study.

Colin Buchanan is Bishop of Woolwich in the diocese of Southwark in the Church of England, and chairman of the Group for Renewal Of Worship.

Introduction

by

PAUL BRADSHAW

There is a theory that every artist has a particular creative work he or she hopes to achieve one day, that every actor is itching for the chance to play Hamlet. Liturgists as such cannot be said to have universally quite the same hopes of engaging with coronations; but the rarity value of coronation events (not least in the lifetime of most living scholars) has accorded study of the rite a sense of entering somewhat solitarily into a rarefied atmosphere—perhaps even a stratosphere—greatly removed from normal liturgical experience. The various persons responsible for Grove Booklets and Liturgical Studies, and for Alcuin Club Monographs and for the present series of Joint Liturgical Studies have at intervals referred to study of coronations as a kind of eschatological joke ('Well, when we have run out of all other subjects, then we can always have a go at coronations . . .'). In part this reflection has had a commercial caution underlying it; for it is difficult to imagine a rush of popular buying even in Britain, and the worldwide readership of this series—not least in various republics, and in many nations far beyond the sovereignty of the English Crown—bids fair to be stolidly unimpressed. Indeed, if we in England were subjected to a study of the rites of inaugurating a kingship of, say, the monarch of an island in the middle of the Pacific, we would classify it as anthropology of strictly limited interest. It may well be that this Study deserves and will receive reciprocal such treatment when catalogued for a library in un-British parts of the world.

The above considerations notwithstanding, the Joint Editorial Board for this series decided that it was neither necessary nor desirable to await either the eschaton or the millennium before engaging with coronation issues. We find ourselves at a point in history interestingly strung between the last coronation and the next. Thus those currently middle-aged had, in so many lives, their first ordinary experience of television when the present Queen was crowned, a shared and memorable experience which means that 2 June 1953 was not simply a watershed for the Queen herself, but was liminal sociologically for millions in these Islands; the younger however are beginning to realize that the question of succession, a question centred in the person of the Prince of Wales, is not infinitely remote but may be upon us any day in any year in the immediate future.

All liturgy carries a message, and a coronation liturgy spells out a relationship of monarch and people, as well as of monarch and God. The rite for each coronation thus far has had considerable continuity with the rite for the preceding coronation, and yet each has had adaptations and, in some cases, even innovations. This rite above all rites cannot be delivered ready-packaged in the way that churchwardens may say to a visiting clergyman at 8 a.m. on a Sunday morning during the incumbent's holiday 'We use the BCP here, without hymns or sermon'. Far from it—the rite is individually tailor-made for each succeeding monarch, whilst also reflecting at times the interest or ignorance or both of Archbishops of Canterbury. But it has to usher in the individual as monarch, and must in some real sense 'fit' him or her. And if, in the intervening period since the last coronation, understandings of monarchy have moved on—or styles of liturgy have moved on—then some discontinuities are likely to appear. We live, on all admissions, in an era when, following the Abdication Crisis in 1936, George VI and Elizabeth II have re-established the throne in people's respect and even awe, not least through their monogamous and faithful family lifestyles—but that respect and awe are currently greatly at risk. What, it is now being asked for the first time, will 'fit' any prospective future monarch?

The present symposium has come together through three different interests arising simultaneously and being brought together between one set of covers. Henry Everett, the minister of Downshire Square, Reading, in 1994 won the Gregory Dix Liturgy Prize, and won it for an essay on that very distinct and paradoxical liturgical occasion, the coronation of James II in 1685. In the process he became well versed in the detail of Tudor and Stuart coronations generally. I myself had recently written on some of the more recent liturgical issues in coronation rites. Colin Buchanan, alone among the Church of England's bishops, has been prepared to stick his neck out against the present establishment of the Church of England, and thus query the somewhat opaque role of the monarch as 'supreme governor' and 'Defender of the Faith'; but, as a liturgist, is also aware of the shape such issues take when written, or not written, into a coronation rite. None of the three of us is committed to views expressed by either of other two, but the interests of each have proved complementary to those of the others, and we hope that the upshot is a story which moves accurately and coherently from historical roots to intense practical realism.

APPENDED NOTE

This Study reached page-proof on 29 August 1997, ready for publication in September. Early in the morning of 31 August 1997, Princess Diana, the divorced ex-wife of Prince Charles, the Prince of Wales, died in a car-crash in Parish. This tragedy made it appropriate to delay publication slightly, and necessitated Colin Buchanan reading his own contribution again and making a few slight alterations. However, the Introduction above has been left as it was drafted prior to the tragedy, and the opening lines of page 34 and the paragraph at the top of page 35 (and its footnote 2—with the pregnant phrase 'contemplating . . . death . . . whilst the present Study is at the press')—all of which reflect on the possible death of the monarch—have also been left as drafted before the Princess' death. The delay of a fotnight has also surprisingly enabled a new footnote 2 to be added on page 37. It is my hope, and that of the other contributors, that both the delay and the slight alterations on the one hand, and the retention of the chapter contents generally in the form in which they were ealier drafted on the other, will be understood and accepted by all those to whom this Study comes.

PFB September 1997

1. The English Coronation Rite: From the Middle Ages to the Stuarts

by
HENRY EVERETT

INTRODUCTION

It might be supposed that a liturgical rite which is seldom performed should remain unchanging through the venerability of age, but in fact the English coronation rite has been altered, if only trivially, on most of the occasions on which it has been performed.[1] Each generation has put its own stamp on the consecration of its monarch, and the rite has been adapted to cope with changed circumstances. The term 'consecration' is used deliberately, because that is without question what the rite is about, whereas 'coronation' refers specifically to a small part of the rite, and by no means the most important. The medieval liturgical books refer always to 'Consecratio Regis' or 'Benedictio Regis' and although the term 'coronation' was current by the seventeenth century the early modern revisers of the rite (who gave the rite the form it has kept through to the twentieth century) were quite clear that this was a consecration they were working on.[2]

In the middle ages the rite was in the custody of the Abbey of Westminster, and it is the Abbey Library which still houses the *Liber Regalis* which is the classic version of the medieval text.[3] The text did, however, evolve over time, possibly through scribal error, but certainly sometimes with deliberate intent. It is important to note that the Tudor monarchs were all consecrated according to the late medieval rite, in Latin, just as their Plantagenet predecessors had been. The rite was put into English first for the consecration of James I, and that translation improved for his son Charles I. The version for Charles I was largely the work of Laud, whose elegant hand can be seen in the Ms copies at St.John's College Cambridge.[4] Laud, bishop of St.David's at the time, was also a prebendary of Westminster, and, since the dean was in disgrace, he was given the responsibility for actually staging the service and acting as master of ceremonies, which was the dean's duty as it had been the abbot's before the Dissolution. The Charles I version was used with only small alterations for Charles II at the Restoration, but controversy had attended the text in the mean time, because it was one of the accusations levelled at Laud during his trial that he had altered the text of both prayers and the coronation oath to produce a more absolutist sense. Modern scholarship has exonerated Laud, but his contemporaries were not so generous.[5]

When James II came to the throne a crisis faced the rite, because he was a Roman Catholic convert, and so might not have consented to the rite being performed at all by Anglican

---

[1] E. C. Ratcliff, *The Coronation Service of Her Majesty Queen Elizabeth II with a Short Historical Introduction, Explanatory Notes and an Appendix* (London, 1953).

[2] See the present author's unpublished MPhil dissertation, R. H. Everett, *The Sacramental Theology of Kingship: A Study on the Persistence of Traditional Theologies of Sovereignty in Early Modern England* (Exeter University, 1995).

[3] W Abb Ms 37.

[4] St. John's Mss L12, L13 and L15.

[5] E. C. Ratcliff, *The English Coronation Service* (London, 1936) pp.128-130.

bishops; in fact a rumour was later reported to the effect that after the ceremony he had sought absolution for the sin of having received anointing at the hands of non-Roman bishops.[1] We might observe that the Stuart kings' belief in 'divine right' was not sufficiently strong to enable them to dispense with the rite of consecration, although they should have believed that they did not need it.[2] James kept the rite, but had it drastically altered, by his loyal archbishop, William Sancroft, so that it was taken out of the context of the eucharist, in which it had always been performed, to avoid the embarrassment of the king not receiving communion. Sancroft's revision was an extremely scholarly one, but the resulting rite was drastically truncated, and by no means the version that Sancroft himself would have chosen.

Unfortunately, Sancroft was the last liturgical scholar to be archbishop of Canterbury, and the last liturgical scholar to be involved in the production of the rite until the mid-twentieth century, and his version exercised a deleterious effect on those which came after it. The rite of 1689, which was drawn up by Henry Compton, bishop of London, using Sancroft's notes, took Sancroft's rite as its point of departure but without much understanding, and has regrettably been the basis for every coronation since. Small amendments have taken place through the intervening three hundred years, but usually the rite has been treated as a mute piece of ceremonial rather than as a living piece of liturgy, and so a number of confusions have been perpetuated, while the striking political theology of the 1680s remains.

MEDIEVAL CORONATIONS

The history of the medieval English coronation rite is not untypical of much medieval liturgy, in that the rite became more elaborate over time and alternatives came to be regarded as complementary.[3] Thus the late fourteenth century rite, which could claim to be the norm, since it remained in use for the best part of three centuries, was hugely longer than its ninth century predecessor.[4] The earliest version of the rite known to us is the so-called 'Egbert' rite, which seems to have been used at the coronation of Queen Judith of Wessex in 856, and which appears in the 'Egbert Pontifical'[5] as well as the Lanalet Pontifical and the Leofric Missal. Professor Ratcliff alleged that it was 'not impossible' that the original form of this rite was the work of Alcuin of York.[6] The rite consists simply of consecratory prayers, the anointing of the king, a series of benedictions, and the delivery of sceptre, rod and crown. After the mass there was a short charge on the three chief duties of a king, plainly the ancestor of the oath.

The second recension of the rite is that used in 973 at the coronation of Edgar, which is sometimes attributed to Dunstan, and which survives in many sources, and which Ratcliff

---

[1] Inside the cover of St. John's Ms L14, which is Sancroft's own copy of the rite that he composed, there is in his hand a note, 'Haerlemse Courant, dated Rome, December 16 1685; Aen seecker prins is Absolutie gesonden van dat hij sig door een Onrooms Bisschop heeft laten salven.'

[2] On divine right see J. N. Figgis CR, *The Divine Right of Kings* (2nd edn. Cambridge, 1914).

[3] The authoritative history of the English rite remains P. E. Schramm, *A History of the English Coronation* (trans. L. G. Wickham Legg) (Oxford, 1937) although some of his conclusions have been questioned.

[4] L. G. Wickham Legg, ed., *English Coronation Records* (London, 1901) (hereafter cited as *ECR*) contains the most easily accessible editions of all the major texts.

[5] W. Greenwell, ed., *The Pontifical of Egbert* (London, Surtees Society, 1853).

[6] Ratcliff *op. cit.* (1936) p.38.

called the Anglo-Saxon Service[1] although it has also been often called the Order of King Ethelred[2] as it was that described by the writer of the *Vita S.Oswaldi* in his account of that king's coronation in 979.[3] This second recension retains all the features of the first but adds others, taken from Roman and French sources, and, most significantly, changes the order of events so that the coronation is now a preliminary to the mass, whereas in 'Egbert' the rite was inserted after the gospel. In this rite the king begins by prostrating himself during the singing of the *Te Deum*, and the election of the king by bishops and people becomes part of the service, and the oath, logically, follows it. Then comes the consecration and anointing, and the king is then invested with ring, sword, crown, sceptre, rod and robe. Finally, after a series of benedictions, he is enthroned, and then the mass is celebrated, with propers that differ from 'Egbert' and are to be found in the *Missa quotidiana pro rege* of the *Gregorian Sacramentary*.[4]

The third recension of the rite dates from the twelfth century, and displays still further Roman influence. It is that which is described by Roger de Hoveden in his account of the coronation of Richard I, and, while it preserves the structure of the Anglo-Saxon rite, it introduces many changes and elaborations, apparently from Roman sources, while omitting some older features. The litany (a Roman feature[5]) appears at the start of the service, during which the king prostrates himself, and then follows the oath and a formal recognition of the king. The benedictions find their way back before the anointing, which seems to be more elaborate than in the earlier rite, since unction on hands, head, breast, shoulders and bends of arms is specified. A second anointing of the head, with chrism rather than ordinary oil, appears. The order in which the ornaments are given changes and the armills appear for the first time; furthermore the ornaments are blessed, the crown specifically. The inthronization follows the king kissing the bishops, and then the mass proceeds.

The fourth recension of the rite, that contained in *Liber Regalis*, which we have called the classic version of the medieval rite, dates from the early fourteenth century, and was first used at the coronation of Edward II in 1308.[6] It combines the previous two recensions, and adds a number of new features as well and is therefore very long indeed. The service begins with the entrance and recognition, but this is separated from the oath by the first oblation and a sermon. New this time are the seven penitential psalms, which follow the litany, and the hymn *Veni Creator*, which precedes it, and the sermon, which precedes the oath. There is also an extra anointing, between the shoulders, and a further elaboration of the ornaments; the king is first dressed in the *colobium sindonis* (a garment rather like an alb) and then the archbishop blesses the regalia in general and invests the king with tunicle, hose and sandals, after which he blesses the sword and invests the king with sword, armills, robe and crown. After the crown comes the ring, separately blessed twice, and the sceptre and rod. After three benedictions and a *Te Deum* the king is enthroned, after which the new feature of nobles doing homage appears.[7] The coronation of the consort would then follow, and the mass then begin, with propers for the occasion and the second oblation at the offertory.

---

[1] ibid. p.39.
[2] R. M. Woolley, *Coronation Rites* (Cambridge, 1915) p.63.
[3] *Historians of the Church of York I* (Rolls Series, 1879) lxxxi p.426.
[4] Woolley, *op. cit.* p.65.
[5] Woolley, *op. cit.* p.67.
[6] For a detailed account of the versions of this recension see A. Hughes, 'The Origins and Descent of the Fourth Recension of the English Coronation' in J. M. Bak (ed.), *Coronations: Medieval and Early Modern Monarchic Ritual* (Berkeley, California, 1990) pp.197-216.
[7] The text of *Liber Regalis* is in *ECR* pp.81-130.

The central section of the rite, the actual consecration of the monarch, is a remarkable conflation in this recension; there are four 'consecratory' prayers, one each from the second and third recensions, as well as two others from other sources, which precede the actual consecration, which is from 'Egbert', but recast into the form of a preface, preceded by the *Sursum corda*. The intention that the king should be consecrated is superabundantly clear, but how and when this occurs is more than a little obscure.

The rite of *Liber Regalis* survived in use, with periodic minor adjustments, for an extraordinarily long time, as we have said, outliving Plantagenets and Tudors, being put into English for the Stuarts and succumbing only in 1685, but we should be cautious about regarding it as the absolute touchstone of the coronation, as Ratcliff did[1], since it is so plainly a conflation rather than a considered construction. As Ratcliff rightly observed, *Liber Regalis* 'is rather the point of departure for, than the ancestor of, the Modern Service'[2] and while it is the most highly developed form of the medieval rite that does not guarantee its liturgical excellence. It is worth pointing out, as Andrew Hughes has demonstrated, that new editions of the rite were not necessarily prepared for specific occasions, and many of the extant copies of the rite of the fourth recension seem to have been compiled simply for reference.[3] Consecratio Regis was a normal item in the contents list of a medieval pontifical, and so orders were copied out whether they were needed or not.

TUDOR AND EARLY STUART CORONATIONS

As we have said, the Tudor monarchs continued to be crowned using the late medieval rite of *Liber Regalis*, and indeed in the case of Henry VII the continuity was such that he used exactly the same manuscript 'little devise of the coronacion' as his predecessor Richard III, with only the names changed.[4] Henry VIII's coronation closely followed that pattern as well, although, unsurprisingly, he wished to alter the coronation oath, but his children each had a different slant on the rite. Edward VI's coronation had a distinctly traditional and catholic appearance,[5] but was distinguished by a sermon by Cranmer which demonstrated a characteristic political theology. The sermon was the most notable contribution of the reformed Church of England to the ancient rite which it had inherited, and it served throughout the early modern period as an important vehicle for the theology of kingship. The rubrics of *Liber Regalis* had required a sermon, directed to be 'short and appropriate' ('congruum breviter sermonem')[6], but in the age of reform this took on an added significance, in the coronation as in any other service. As the rite itself was left untouched, so the sermon gained importance for the expression of the theory which underpinned it. Cranmer's sermon, as Richard McCoy has pointed out, 'preached a thoroughly Protestant view of the liturgy and kingship'[7] declaring the oil to be but a ceremony, and the king to be a perfect monarch whether or not he was anointed.

In outward appearance and liturgical substance Mary Tudor's coronation was virtually identical to her brother's, although she did send to the Emperor for some newly consecrated chrism.[8] The question of the chrism is an enduring one in the history of the rite, and is

---

[1] See his introduction to his own revision of the modern rite; Ratcliff, *op. cit.*. (1953) *passim*.
[2] Ratcliff, *op. cit.* (1936) p.40.
[3] Hughes, *op. cit.* p.210.
[4] B. L. Egerton Ms 985, f.1. Text in *ECR* pp.220.239.
[5] See the Ely Ms account reproduced by Ratcliff, *op. cit.* (1936) pp.111-115.
[6] *ECR* p.87.
[7] R. C. McCoy, '"The Wonderful Spectacle" The Civic Progress of Elizabeth I and the Troublesome Coronation' in J. M. Bak (ed.), *op. cit.* p.218.
[8] *Idem.*

worth examining here. As we have said, chrism (as opposed to the oil of catechumens) is first used in the third recension of the English rite, and for two hundred years it is simply that which is consecrated along with the other oils on Maundy Thursday, but in the fourteenth century the story of the miraculous oil appears, and thereafter it is this special, allegedly miraculous, chrism which is used. The story first appears in a letter from Pope John XXII to Edward II, and alleges that this chrism was given by the Virgin Mary to Thomas Becket, who ordered a monk to hide it until a convenient time.[1] The story is plainly the counterpart of the French story of the 'Sainte Ampoulle' (brought by a dove from heaven to St.Remigius) of the same period, part of the two monarchies' battle for prestige. Whatever its origin, this miraculous chrism was used for all English coronations until Edward VI. Mary had hers newly consecrated, but Elizabeth used some already existing. Some have assumed that this was the miraculous chrism, as she is reported to have said that 'the grease smelt ill'[2] but it might equally have been that consecrated for Mary, or that consecrated on Maundy Thursday 1558. There is no record of new chrism for James I, so we should assume that it was preserved for him, and indeed Prynne reported that he was anointed with 'the Oyle with which antiently the Kings and Queens have been anointed'[3] but Laud's preparations for Charles I's coronation included the creation and consecration of new chrism. What happened in 1661 is not clear, but it is certain new chrism must have been consecrated, presumably using Laud's recipe and form of consecration. In 1685 Sancroft had new chrism made up and consecrated it on the morning of the service, but in 1689 the chrism was blessed during the coronation. That remarkable departure from precedent happened only once, and it is plain that thereafter the Chapter of Westminster usually guarded the old chrism, but that sometimes it was consecrated anew. Woolley states that it was 'certainly consecrated beforehand for the anointing of George II'[4] while Jocelyn Perkins reports the consecration of new chrism using Sancroft's forms by Bishop Welldon in 1902, and its subsequent use in 1911 and 1937.[5]

Elizabeth I's coronation poses a number of questions, because while the rite followed is certain enough, the actions of the queen and the identities of some of the participants are not clear, and Richard McCoy has examined it in some detail.[6] The rite was that of *Liber Regalis*, in Latin, exactly in the medieval manner, performed as an introduction to the mass. The rite expressed political and ecclesiastical continuity and legitimacy.

For James I the rite was at last put into English, 'drawn in haste' according to Heylin[7], and omitting the seven penitential psalms. Ratcliff charitably attributes the omission of phrases from the oath to that haste[8], but since the omissions tended to extend the royal prerogative we might take a different point of view. We should always bear in mind the political importance of the coronation in the early modern period; the origin of sovereignty and the nature of sovereignty were at the heart of political debate, so the coronation was a political event, dramatizing a political theology.

The sermon was once again what was remembered about Charles I's coronation, in ,1626, as it was preached on the text 'Be thou faithful unto death, and I will give thee a crown of life' (Rev. 2.10) which came to be regarded as a portent.[9] As we have said, Laud's

---

[1] *ECR* pp.69 ff.
[2] J. Perkins, *The Crowning of the Sovereign* (2nd edn, London, 1953) p.107.
[3] *Idem*.
[4] Woolley, *op. cit.*, p.89.
[5] Perkins, *op. cit.*, pp. 108-109. See also J. Perkins, *Sixty Years at Westminster Abbey* (London, 1960) p.39.
[6] McCoy, *op. cit.*, pp.217-227.
[7] R. Heylin, *Cyprianus Anglicus* (London, 1671) p.145.
[8] Ratcliff, *op. cit.*, (1936) p.121.
[9] C. Wordsworth, ed., *The Manner of the Coronation of King Charles I* (London, 1892) p.18.

part in the preparation of the service came to be one of the grounds on which he was tried, the apparent extension of the royal prerogative being the issue. Liturgically the rite was little changed from 1603, although Heylin records that Laud's revision of it was supposed 'to accomodate the same more punctually to the present Rules and Orders of the Church of England'.[1] In fact, if the two rites are examined it will be seen that nothing of substance has changed; the medieval liturgy was found to accomodate quite punctually to the Stuart Church of England.[2]

One feature of Charles I's coronation which is worthy of note is that his consort, Henrietta Maria, was never crowned. Although it has always been customary for English consorts to be crowned and anointed, it is by no means necessary, either theologically or politically, and of course male consorts have never been either crowned or anointed. The modern rite prays that the consort may be made a 'great example of virtue and piety, and a blessing to the kingdom' and that the anointing will increase her honour and that by it the grace of the Holy Spirit will establish her. The stress has always been on the consort simply as an example of virtue, and the anointing as conferring the grace necessary to be such an example. Since the consort does not have to rule, there is much less sense of her needing grace than there is for the actual monarch, who needs to be strengthened by God for the exercise of his role in society. It has been normal for female consorts to be crowned, but the consorts of Richard I, Charles II, George I and George IV are all further exceptions, while Henry VIII gave up having his wives crowned after Anne Boleyn at Pentecost 1533. In the case of Henrietta Maria, it was believed that the king intended that she should be crowned but that she declined, as Sancroft put it 'for reasons easy to be conjectured.(Ye Eucharist)'.[3] Certainly the draft of the rite included the queen's coronation, but it was not in the end performed.

Charles II's coronation was the last using the order of *Liber Regalis*, and it adhered closely to that used for his father. As we have observed, his queen was not crowned. All the regalia and robes had to be made anew, which was a considerable expense[4], and of course Westminster was provided with its famous copes for the occasion. Among the regalia there was made an orb, which caused Sancroft some problems a quarter century later, because he, or one of his colleagues, seems to have felt obliged to find it a role in the service, which, since the orb is only actually a sceptre of a different shape, was difficult. In Sancroft's draft of the rite the orb does not originally appear and the robe is given to the king alone, but then he has added in the orb, though without altering the accompanying sentence.[5] In the final version, however, it seems to have been once more called into question, as there is a marginal note 'q of ye Orb' when it appears with the robe[6], but then it seems to have been quite forgotten, since its return to the archbishop is an addition to the original text.[7] The consensus is that the orb and sceptre are the same item, but there was certainly an orb in the regalia before the Civil War, since there is a gold 'globe' listed straight after the crowns in the Parliamentary Inventory of the Regalia in 1649[8], and an orb appears in more than

---

[1] Heylin, *op. cit.*, p.145, quoted in Ratcliff 1936 p.123..
[2] Both orders are printed in Wordsworth, *op. cit.*
[3] Tanner Mss. 31:96.
[4] See the list of 'Necessaries to be Provided' in *ECR* p.277.
[5] Tanner Mss. 31.106.
[6] St.John's Coll. Ms L14 leaf 38. (Wrongly noted in *ECR* p.302).
[7] *Ibid.* leaf 40. (*ECR* p.304).
[8] *ECR* p.273.

one portrait of Charles I (for instance the 1631 portrait by Daniel Mytens in the National Portrait Gallery).[1] It seems curious that an item of regalia should exist for which there was no purpose, so we can forgive Sancroft for finding a use for a new one manufactured at some expense.

THE CORONATIONS OF THE 1680S

When William Sancroft revised the rite in 1685 he was under instructions 'to take out the communion service and to abridge (as much as conveniently might be) the extreme length of the rest preserving notwithstanding the forme of the Coronation Oath (and other the most essential things) unaltered and exactly the same as they stood in the offices of the coronations of King Charles the first and King Charles the second of blessed memory.'[2] That he carried out these instructions to the satisfaction of his monarch (or, as Jocelyn Perkins put it, satisfied 'the king's Romanist scruples')[3] is evident from the fact that his service was authorized by the royal warrant of 21 April 1685 which records these instructions. It was plainly a radical departure from precedent to detach the consecration of the monarch from the eucharist, but by no means an unusual one for the period, as the rites of Bohemia (1619), Scotland (1651), Denmark (1559), Sweden (1675) and Prussia (1701) demonstrate.[4] Ironically, those were all definitely Protestant monarchies, whereas James's problem was precisely his Roman Catholicism, and it is clear that a royal consecration outside the eucharist was the characteristic of a Protestant state.[5] The fact that Sancroft was able to effect the change demonstrates the adaptability of the ancient rite, although Sancroft himself was in no doubt that the change was a mistake: 'the Archbp should immediately begin THE COMMUNION' he wrote in one of his drafts.[6] For Sancroft the continuity of the rite was important, and he had no desire to seem to be endorsing a Protestant (as opposed to Anglican) state. As we shall see, he strove hard to maintain the sacramental sense of the rite, and to make its meaning clearer in ways that can hardly be called Protestant.

Sancroft was thorough in his work of abbreviation, although not necesarily entirely consistent. The 1626 rite, which was his starting point, contains thirty prayers and formulae; Sancroft's rite reduces these to twenty-two. Of those twenty-two only two are significantly longer than their 1626 counterparts (*Deus Humilium* at the first oblation, and the final benediction), while one more (*Deus Dei Filius* at the anointing) is slightly longer. Of the remaining nineteen prayers or formulae, nine are shorter than their counterparts, three of them quite dramatically so (*Omnipotens Sempiterne Deus* after the litany, the preface over the oil and the formula at the delivery of the sceptre). Where the length of prayers remains virtually the same Sancroft has usually made some small alterations in the wording, and it is in his tiny alterations that his intention can best be seen. Curiously, he added remarkably few new phrases of his own to existing prayers, rather he worked mostly by conflating existing texts, but where we can identify his own words they tell a striking story.

---

[1] Reproduced in Sir Roy Strong, *Lost Treasures of Britain* (London, 1990) pp.120-121.
[2] Tanner Mss. 31:31.
[3] Perkins, *op. cit.* p.9.
[4] Woolley, *op. cit.* pp.137-158.
[5] Contrary to the view of L. G. Schwoerer, who mistakes the nature of seventeenth century Anglicanism.
   L. G. Schwoerer, 'The Coronation of William and Mary, April 11, 1689' in L. G. Schwoerer, ed., *The Revolution of 1688-9; Changing Perspectives* (Cambridge, 1992) pp.107-130.
[6] Tanner Mss.31:75.

Sancroft recast all the blessings of the regalia in the 1626 rite to be blessings of the king (an action which Ratcliff seems to have regarded as eccentric and unforgivable)[1] which was simply bringing the rite into conformity with contemporary Anglican practice, since nowhere in the Book of Common Prayer is an object blessed (not even the water of baptism). It was curious that the blessings survived in 1626, but Sancroft carefully changed them all (except in the case of the ring) into blessings of the king who was about to wear them. We might observe that in the late twentieth century the Roman Catholic Church has largely moved away from the blessing of objects to the blessing of those who wear, bear, or use them, which has always been the majority practice in Anglicanism. Sancroft may or may not have been right to have departed from medieval forms in this, but he was certainly not following some particular whim of his own, as Professor Ratcliff would have us believe. In his version of *Deus Tuorum*, the former blessing of the crown, we can see, in a tiny phrase, a clue to Sancroft's attitude. In the 1626 rite *Deus Tuorum* runs:

God the crowne of ye faithfull, who crownest their heads wth a crowne of precious stones, that trust in thee, Blesse and sanctify this Crowne, that as ye same is adorned with diverse precious stones, so this thy servant that weareth it, mau be filled wth thy manifold graces of all pretious vertues through. . . .[2]

Sancroft's version, while retaining the point of the prayer, that the king be granted grace and virtue, differs in a small but significant phrase:

O God, ye Crown of ye Faithfull, Bless, we beseech thee, and sanctify this thy servant, James our King; And as thou do'st this Day set a Crown of pure Gold upon his Head; so enrich his Roial Heart wth thine abundant Grace, and Crown him wth all princely Vertues, through . . .[3]

With the addition of the phrase 'thou do'st this Day' we can see Sancroft making a point about the nature of kingship and the function of coronations. It is plain that both these prayers are for the increase of God's grace on the king, but in his version Sancroft makes two points: that it is on this day that the king truly becomes king, and that it is God who makes him king. Both are important points and make sense when we consider what we know of Sancroft's political philosophy, for he is here implicitly denying the notion of indefeasible divine right, that the king is monarch simply by virtue of his birth, by insisting that it is at the coronation that the king truly becomes king. On the other hand, Sancroft makes it plain that it is God who bestows kingship and kingly authority, and not anyone here on earth; although elements of election remain in the rite, the early medieval idea of the king's authority coming from the consent of the assembled notables[4] has no place in Sancroft's scheme. For Sancroft, James II is king by divine authority, but that authority is bestowed in the coronation rite.

Lest it be thought that this is a large conceptual edifice to build on one small phrase, which after all simply states a fact, that the king is actually crowned at his coronation, we need now to examine seven other amendments of Sancroft's, which while small in themselves build into a substantial cumulative case. Let us turn first to the prayer *Te Invocamus*, the collect following the *Veni Creator*, which in its 1626 version runs thus:

. . . thou wilt evermore enrich him wth the gifts of piety, fulfill him wth the grace of truth & encrease him daily in all goodness in the sight of God & men, that he may ioyfully receive the state of supreme Government by the gift of thy supernaturall grace. . . .[5]

---

[1] Ratcliff, *op. cit.* (1953) p.14.
[2] St. John's Coll. Ms. L15. In Wordsworth, *op. cit.* p.39.
[3] St. John's Coll. Ms. L14, leaf 39 (*ECR* p.303). My underlining.
[4] See eg. J. L. Nelson, 'Hincmar of Reims on King-making' in J. M. Bak, ed., *op. cit.* pp.16-34.
[5] St. John's Coll. Ms. L15. In Wordworth, *op. cit.* p.27.

Sancroft's version of the same prayer reads:

> . . . thou wouldst enrich him evermore with thy Bounty, and fill him with Grace, and Truth, and daily encrease in him all Goodness in ye sight of God, and Man: That being placed in ye throne of Supreme Government, assisted with thy heavenly Grace, and by thy Mercy defended from all his Enemies, he may govern ye people committed to his charge. . . .[1]

Sancroft has made the sequence of events in the thought of the collect much clearer: the king is to be enriched, filled and daily increased, so that being placed in the throne, assisted and defended, he may govern. This is quite different from the Caroline version where the king's joyfully receiving the 'state' of government seems dependent on his being enriched, fulfilled and increased. For Sancroft the enrichment is a future prayer, but being placed in the throne is something that is happening now, at the coronation. It is also worth noting that 'being placed' is quite different from 'receiving': the bishops place the king in his throne, he does not just receive it directly from the Almighty.

The next of the prayers in the Caroline rite, *Omnipotens et Sempiterne Deus*, which follows the litany, contains the phrase:

> . . . multiply thy blessings upon this thy Servant Charles, whome in lowly devotion we consecrate our King. . . .[2]

Sancroft prunes the prayer drastically, adding very little new material, but in his version this phrase reads:

> . . . multiply thy Blessings upon this thy Servant James; whom in thy Name wth lowly Devotion we are about to consecrate Our King. . . .[3]

The phrase 'are about to' appears in Sancroft's draft as a late marginal addition, but it serves to make the temporal sequence clear: at this point in the service James II is not yet a consecrated king, but is about to become one. Looking simply at the rite, this would seem to imply very clearly that it is the anointing which consecrates the king, and not the prayers beforehand (of which this is one) which were four in number in 1626 (and of course in *Liber Regalis*) but which were reduced to two by Sancroft. It seems that Sancroft associates the consecration of the king with the sacramental act of anointing, which has not yet taken place at this point, rather than with any form of words. Certainly it is the rite itself which will consecrate the king, on this day and in this place.

The prayer which accompanies the anointing, then, is that which is consecratory for Sancroft. In his rite, as in its predecessors, this prayer has the form of a eucharistic preface, preceded by the *Sursum corda*, which elevates its solemnity. Sancroft seeks to excise phrases in his version which imply a consecratory power in the oil itself, but if anything he heightens the importance of the anointing itself, and certainly draws attention to the bishops' role in it. The 1626 version of the prayer reads:

> . . . Wee beseech thee, almighty Father, that by ye Fatnesse of this thy Creature thou wilt vouchsafe to blesse and sanctify this thy Servant Charles, that in the simplicity of a dove he may minister peace unto his people; that he may imitate Aaron in ye service of God; that he may attaine the perfection of Government in Counsell and Iudgement and that by the anointing of this Oile thou maist give him a countenance alwaies cheerfull and amiable to ye whole people. . . .[4]

---

[1] St. John's Coll. Ms. L14. leaf 33 (*ECR* p.298). My underlining.
[2] St. John's Coll. Ms. L15. In Wordsworth, *op. cit.* pp.27-29.
[3] St. John's Coll. Ms. L14, leaf 27 (*ECR* p.295). My underlining.
[4] St. John's Coll. Ms. L15. In Wordsworth, *op. cit.* pp.30-31.

Sancroft's version is more direct, and crucially different:

> We beseech thee to bless, and sanctify this thy Servant James our King now to be anointed wth holy Oil by Our Office, and Ministry; And plenteously to endue him wth all ye Gifts and Graces of thy holy Spirit, wch thou didst of old confer upon thy chosen servants by this Ministry. . . .[1]

One may lament Sancroft's removal of colourful phrases (though not the infelicitous 'Aaron' clause) but his meaning is clear; that royal anointing in Stuart England is equivalent to the anointing of 'Kings, priests, and prophets' in ancient Israel, and that it is God's ministers, in this case the bishops of the Church of England, who mediate that action. The anointing is explicitly connected with the 'Gifts and Graces' of the Holy Spirit, which is a major advance in the clarity of the rite, and incidentally makes a pleasing connection with initiatory chrismation, which is surely the liturgical precedent for coronation anointing.[2] Grosseteste had made a comparison between coronation anointing and confirmation in the thirteenth century, in a famous answer to a question from Henry III, and that opinion may have been well known in the late seventeenth century, as John Selden had quoted it in his *Titles of Honour*[3], so it is possible that Sancroft found his inspiration there. In any event, it is now clear that this anointing is about the bestowal of the gifts of the Holy Spirit, in order that a monarch may reign well, and that this happens through the ministry of the Church. This emphasis of Sancroft's has remained untouched.

Sancroft's finding the precedent for coronation anointing in confirmation (rather than in ordination) is possibly also responsible for his transfer of the main prayer accompanying the anointings from the anointing of the hands to the anointing of the head, although it is also more liturgically satisfactory at that point[4], but he also made a small but significant alteration to the substance of that text. In 1626 the hands were anointed first with the prayer:

> Let these handes be anointed wth holy Oile, as Kings and Prophets have been anointed, and as Samuel did anoint David to be king, that thou mai'st be blessed and established king . . .[5]

while in 1685 the head was anointed last with the prayer:

> Be this Head anointed with holy Oil; as kings and prophets were anointed. And as Solomon was anointed king by Zadok ye priest, and Nathan ye Prophet; so be thou anointed, blessed and establish'd King . . .[6]

which strikingly changes the biblical example, from the charismatic prophet marking out a king from a completely new dynasty to the representatives of official religion consecrating a legitimate heir. This is obviously a significant political point for Sancroft to have made, though it might also be said that it makes more sense of the traditional singing of the anthem 'Zadok the Priest' (in pre-Handelian form, to a setting by Henry Lawes in this case)[7] at this point as well.

---

[1] St. John's Coll. Ms. L14, leaf 34 (*ECR* p.299). My underlining.
[2] See J. L. Nelson, *Politics and Ritual in Early Medieval Europe* (London, 1986) pp.239ff. Also J. D. Crichton, 'Unction' in J. G. Davies, ed., *A Dictionary of Liturgy and Worship* (London, 1972) pp.358-360.
[3] J. Wickham Legg, *Three Coronation Orders* (London, 1900) p.142.
[4] See R. H. Everett, *op. cit.* pp.57-59 for an extended discussion.
[5] St. John's Coll. Ms. L15. In Wordsworth, *op. cit.* p.32.
[6] St. John's Coll. Ms. L14 leaf 35. (*ECR* p.300).
[7] Sir W. McKie, 'Music in the Abbey' in E. Carpenter, ed., *A House of Kings: The History of Westminster Abbey* (London, 1966) p.436.

There is also a tiny change in the wording of the address at the delivery of the ring. In 1626 it runs:

> Receive the Ring of kingly Dignity, and by it ye Seale of Catholique faith, yt as this day thou art adorned ye Head and Prince of this Kingdome . . .[1]

while Sancroft's version is as follows:

> Receive ye Ring of kingly Dignity, and the Seal of Catholick Faith: that as thou art this Day consecrated Head, and Prince of this Kingdom . . .[2]

which makes explicit that the king is being consecrated and not simply adorned (the Latin of Liber Regalis has 'ornaris'). For Sancroft a sacramental action is taking place, in which the king is consecrated, and, while this was of course the assumption underlying the medieval rite, it was far from clear in the old texts, and so Sancroft clarifies it for his audience. He does not take the opportunity to express some modern doctrine of sovereignty, or even avail himself of honourable Anglican ambiguity, but actually makes more explicit in the rite a traditional understanding of kingship and kingly consecration.

At the delivery of the sceptre and the rod Sancroft weaves together existing texts artfully and adds one phrase of his own which we might note:

> . . . assist thee in ye Administration of that Dignity, wch he hath given thee . . .[3]

which tends to establish a 'moment of consecration' for the king, who has just been given, by God, the dignity of kingship at the anointing.

The final one of Sancroft's amendments is from the prayer *Sta et Retine* at the inthronization, which in 1626 read:

> Stand and hold fast from henceforth that place whereof hitherto you have been heire by ye succession of your forefathers, being now delivered unto you by the Authority of Almighty God, and by ye hands of us and all the Bishops and Servants of God . . .[4]

Sancroft improves the English and makes two points:

> Stand firm, and hold fast from henceforth yt Place of Roial Dignity, whereof thou art ye lawfull, and undoubted Heir by Succession from thy Forefathers; and wch hath been this Day delivered unto thee in ye Name, and by ye Auctority of Almighty God, and by ye hands of Us, ye Bishops, and Servants of God . . .[5]

The first point is that to call James II 'lawfull, and undoubted' heir is to make a very topical political statement; it was simply not true that James was undoubted, as that was what the Exclusion Crisis was all about. The second point is that Sancroft emphasizes once again the timing of the delivery of James's royal dignity, which may have been less palatable to the king. The 1626 rite has a continuous present, 'being now delivered' while Sancroft uses the perfect tense, 'hath been this Day delivered' which is far more emphatic. For Sancroft and his attentive listeners there can be no question; it is at the coronation that the king receives his kingly dignity when he is consecrated by anointing with holy oil at the hands of the bishops. God gives the king authority, and the grace to exercise that authority, and he does that through the sacramental ministry of the country's catholic bishops.

Sancroft refused to have anything to do with William and Mary after the revolution of 1688-9, remaining faithful to his oath of allegiance to James, and so he did not crown the new monarchs, Henry Compton, bishop of London, (and James's least favourite prelate) acting in his stead, but Sancroft's hand can be seen behind the altered rite. Compton wrote

---

[1] St. John's Coll. Ms. L15. In Wordsworth, *op. cit.*, p.41.
[2] St. John's Coll. Ms. L14 leaf 41. (*ECR* pp.304-305)
[3] St. John's Coll. Ms. L14 leaf 41. (*ECR* p.305).
[4] St. John's Coll. Ms. L15. In Wordsworth, *op. cit.*, p.45.
[5] St. John's Coll. Ms. L14 leaf 44. (*ECR* p.307).

to Sancroft asking for his coronation notes, and it is plain that he received them.[1] It was necessary to put the coronation back into the context of the eucharist (so that no other Roman Catholic could do as James had done) but, rather than return to the format of *Liber Regalis* with the coronation as an extended introductory rite, Compton inserted the coronation into the eucharist after the liturgy of the word, simply following Sancroft's draft.[2]

Sancroft's connection of coronation anointing with initiatory chrismation had an effect on Compton's rite as well, as it resulted in a portion of the Prayer Book confirmation prayer finding its way into the central prayer at the anointing (which had been in the form of a preface). Compton dispensed with a separate blessing of chrism, and instead blessed it openly in that central prayer, which he constructed out of Sancroft's 'preface' combined with his blessing of the chrism, along with the section of the 1662 confirmation prayer spelling out those 'gifts and graces of the Holy Spirit'.[3] Strikingly, not only did Compton openly bless the chrism (an innovation which did not last, although absurdly the rubric for it was still there in 1953) but he strengthened the language of consecration, introducing the word 'consecrated' into two of the prayers at the anointing. Sancroft had clarified the question, and Compton followed him in stressing the notion of consecration, which strikingly illustrates his political theology. It is certainly to Compton's credit, as Ratcliff remarked, that in a time of revolution the notion of the consecration of the monarch was not allowed to disappear[4], and indeed was emphasized still further.

Of Sancroft's amendments that we have noted, most remained untouched by Compton, so the moment of consecration of the monarch remained firmly established (although two of those prayers simply disappeared), but Compton's order certainly did not clarify what was going on. As it remained the norm for the next two hundred and fifty years it is worth describing. The order begins with the royal entry, which is followed by the recognition, the first oblation (of a gold pall and an ingot of gold) and the litany with its accompanying collect. Then the Prayer Book communion service begins, and proceeds up to the creed, after which the sermon is preached. Then the oath is administered, and, after *Veni Creator* is sung, the consecratory prayer (the former 'preface') is said and the monarch anointed. Compton reduced the anointings to three, and curiously inverted the order so that, the king's head was anointed first, rather than as the climax. A collect concludes the anointing and then the regalia are presented; first the monarch is clothed in *colobium sindonis* and tunicle, and then spurs, sword, armill, robe, orb, ring, sceptre, rod and crown are presented. After the crowning the Bible is presented, Compton's innovation and in a very odd place, since it is not an item of regalia. Then comes the benediction, followed by a *Te Deum*, then the inthronization which is followed by the homage. The rite returns to the Prayer Book eucharist at the offertory, when the second oblation (of bread and wine and a purse of gold) is made, accompanied by an offertory prayer, Sancroft's rendering of one of the secrets from *Liber Regalis*.[5] The monarch and consort receive communion along with the officiating clergy, and a final prayer is inserted into the conclusion of the eucharist.

Ironically, Compton lengthened much of the text he had inherited from Sancroft, but his prolixity was gradually cut down in subsequent versions, although nothing of substance was changed until 1902 and Professor Ratcliff's revision for 1953. Hence the political theology of the late seventeeth century found repeated liturgical expression for over two hundred years, and monarchs continued to be consecrated in a rite that, while radically different in shape from its medieval predecessors, yet clearly retained its sacramental purpose.

---

[1] Tanner Mss. 27:8.
[2] Tanner Mss. 31:75.
[3] *ECR* p.327.
[4] Ratcliff, *op. cit.*, (1953) p.16.
[5] Tanner Mss. 31:75.

Appendix to Chapter 1

ILLUSTRATIONS OF THE CORONATION OF JAMES II

Sideways on, reproduced on pages 20 and 21 overleaf,are two illustrations of the coronation of James II. These are taken from Francis Sandford, *The History of the Coronation of
King James II* (London, 1687), kept in the library of Westminster Abbey.

Page 20 Ground-plan of the Abbey.

Page 21 Perspective looking west.

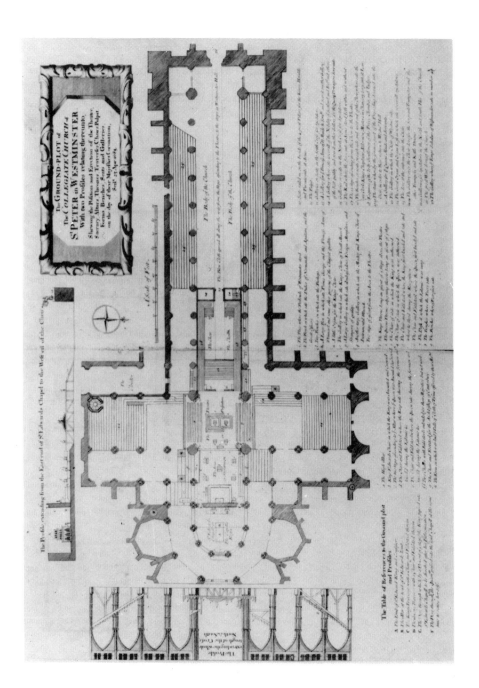

A Perspective of WESTMINSTER Abby from the High Altar to the West [...] the Manner of [...] H.s Majesty Charles 2nd

W. Brown sculp

2. Coronations from the Eighteenth to the Twentieth Century

by

PAUL BRADSHAW

THE EIGHTEENTH AND NINETEENTH CENTURIES

From the coronation of William and Mary in 1689 until the coronation of Queen Victoria in 1838 changes in the rite were relatively few, apart of course from the disappearance of the 'joint' character of that particular occasion. Queen Anne was crowned on 23 April 1702—St. George's Day. Her state of health did not permit her to make the journey from Westminster Hall to the Abbey on foot, as had been customary, and so she was carried 'in an open Chair, with a Canopy of Yellow Velvet, supported by several of the barons of the Cinque Ports, carried over it, the Crown, Sceptre and Globe lying on a Velvet Cushion before Her . . .'[1] Within the service itself, the only significant changes were one addition and two deletions. The addition was the inclusion of a Declaration against Transubstantiation, Invocation of Saints, and the Sacrifice of the Mass to be made by the sovereign before taking the Oath, intended of course to exclude a Roman Catholic from the throne. One of the deletions was the petition 'bless this oil' from the prayer at the anointing, even though the rubric which had accompanied it still remained: *'Here the Archbishop is to lay his hand upon the Ampulla.'* The petition and rubric had been inserted at the coronation of William and Mary, and their removal meant that the sovereign was now to be hallowed with unhallowed oil.[2] The other deletion was the girding on of the Sword at the presentation of the royal regalia, even though previous Queens (Elizabeth I, Mary I, Mary II) had been girded with it. The Sword was still presented to her, but the reference to girding in the accompanying prayer was omitted, and the same procedure was also followed in the case of Victoria and of Elizabeth II.

The coronation services of George I (20 October 1714) and George II (11 October 1727) did not differ in any significant respects from that of Queen Anne, except that in the case of George II the rite for the coronation of a Queen was included. The coronation of George III (22 September 1761), which also involved the coronation of his Queen, married just two weeks beforehand, is notable for the many small changes that were made in the wording of the rite (none of any great significance), for the inclusion of ten anthems, and for the fact that the King did not put on two of the traditional garments after the anointing—the *Colobium Sindonis* (a sort of alb) and the *Supertunica* (a tunicle made of cloth of gold). Although these had not been mentioned in the rubrics of the rite from the revision made for William and Mary onwards, it is known that they did continue to be worn at that and all succeeding coronations, and that they were made in readiness for the coronation of George III. Why they were not actually used on the occasion remains a mystery.

---

[1] *London Post* no. 454, quoted from E. C. Ratcliff, *The English Coronation Service* (SPCK, London, 1937), p.137.

[2] The claim made by F. C. Eeles, *The Coronation Service: Its Meaning and History* (Mowbray, London, 1952), p.32, that 'since the time of William and Mary the oil has been blessed during the service, just before the anointing' is thus clearly a misunderstanding.

The coronation of George IV (19 July 1821) is noteworthy not so much for the ceremony itself as for the sumptuousness of the surrounding processions and entertainments. However, these spectacles apparently failed to arouse corresponding feelings of popularity among his subjects. According to a contemporary writer, 'the coronation of George IV, though the most gorgeous pageant ever exhibited in England, excited far less enthusiasm in the public generally, than that of any of his predecessors'.[1] The lack of popular enthusiasm may have been in part due to the King's refusal to allow his estranged wife Caroline of Brunswick to be crowned as Queen with him. Although she presented herself at the Abbey on the day in defiance of his command, she was denied entry and forced to withdraw in humiliation. In the rite itself, it is reported that the King was anointed on the hands and head only, the unction of the breast being omitted, even though printed in the order of service.[2] This alteration may have had something to do with the delicacy of the age, and it was repeated at the other nineteenth-century coronations. Also on this occasion the Declaration against Transubstantiation, Invocation of the Saints, and the Sacrifice of the Mass was removed from the service and made instead before both Houses of Parliament. This continued to be the practice until the coronation of George V, when by the Accession Declaration Act of 1910, the sovereign has since then only been required to declare before Parliament that he or she is 'a faithful Protestant'.

The coronation of William IV (8 September 1831) was in marked contrast to that of his elder brother and predecessor. Public opinion was antipathetic towards any extravagant expenditure on the event, and the King therefore directed that 'no ceremonies are to be celebrated at the Coronation, except the sacred rites attending the administration of the royal oath in Westminster Abbey. The usual procession and feast are to be dispensed with'.[3] His description of the service as 'the sacred rites attending the administration of the royal oath' reveals a strange perspective on the occasion, considering that in reality the Oath is but a preliminary to the anointing and investiture, which constitute the true heart of the rite. The omission of the public procession from Westminster Hall to the Abbey was the cause of considerable regret to contemporary commentators, and necessitated the erection of a retiring room at the west entrance to the Abbey, in which the King and Queen robed after their journey from St. James' Palace in the State Coach. A similar practice has been followed at all subsequent coronations. Although the editor of *The Times* desired the abridgement of a great part of the coronation ritual as 'compounded of the worst dregs of popery and feudalism'[4], only a few small changes were made in the service itself, among them—as indicated above—the omission of the anointing of the breast in the case of both King and Queen. Also in contrast to tradition, the Sword, although still presented to the King, was not girded upon him; the King and Queen removed their crowns for the reception of Holy Communion; and a houselling-cloth of silk or linen was no longer held before them during the reception of the sacrament. This traditional custom has not since been revived.

The relatively simple coronation arrangements of 1831 were largely repeated for the coronation of Queen Victoria on 28 June 1838, but, in order to satisfy popular demand for

---

[1] *Chapters on Coronations* (London, 1838), p.197. The anonymous author is thought to have been William Cooke Taylor.

[2] William Maskell, *Monumenta Ritualia Ecclesiae Anglicanae* III (W. Pickering, London, 1847), p.108.

[3] *London Gazette*, 10 July, 1831.

[4] Quoted from *The Gentleman's Magazine*, 1 September 1831.

something more stately, 'the exterior cavalcade was increased in splendour and numbers, and a much more extended line of approach was adopted'.[1] In the service[2], the Queen wore the *Colobium Sindonis* and the *Supertunica* throughout, and so was not invested with them after the anointing, and, in the well-known painting of the coronation by C. R. Leslie, these garments look less like the conventional alb and tunicle and more like a ball-gown with the skirt parted to show a petticoat underneath. Moreover, not only was the anointing of the breast omitted, but the ancient tradition of the sovereign kissing the bishops after the Benediction and before the Inthroning was omitted, and has never been restored since; and those doing Homage at the end kissed the Queen's hand rather than her cheek. These variations were no doubt occasioned by the reserve of the period towards outward shows of intimacy.

A contemporary description gives the lie to the common English myth that we have always been good at organizing ceremonial and pageantry. That skill turns out to be a much more recent development:

'The different actors in the ceremonial were very imperfect in their parts, and had neglected to rehearse them. Lord John Thynne, who officiated for the Dean of Westminster, told me that nobody knew what was to be done except the Archbishop and himself (who had rehearsed), Lord Willoughby (who is experienced in these matters), and the Duke of Wellington, and consequently there was continual difficulty and embarrassment, and the Queen never knew what she was to do next. They made her leave her chair and enter into St. Edward's Chapel before the prayers were concluded, much to the discomforture of the Archbishop. She said to John Thynne, "Pray tell me what I am to do, for they don't know"; and at the end, when the orb was put into her hand, she said to him, "What am I to do with it?" "Your Majesty is to carry it, if you please, in your hand.". "Am I?" she said' "it is very heavy." The ruby ring was made for her little finger instead of the fourth, on which the rubric prescribes that it should be put. When the Archbishop was to put it on, she extended the former, but he said it must be on the latter. She said it was too small, and she could not get it on. He said it was right to put it there, and, as he insisted, she yielded, but had first to take off her other rings, and then this was forced on, but it hurt her very much . . .'.[3]

If such could be the chaos and confusion when the previous coronation had been held only seven years earlier, imagine what it must have been like when a much greater interval had elapsed and memories had grown even more dim!

THE CORONATION OF EDWARD VII

Such a lengthy interval did of course occur between the coronation of Queen Victoria and that of Edward VII in 1902. In this case matters were complicated still further by the fact that the King became ill and had to undergo an operation for appendicitis, necessitating the postponement of the event from 26 June, the King's birthday, until 9 August, when he was judged well enough to take part. Nevertheless, it was not marred by the same confusion that had affected Victoria's coronation, and as Peter Hinchliff has recently pointed out, there was now both a liturgical interest and a liturgical expertise that had not existed in the

---

[1] *The Gentleman's Magazine*, August 1838.
[2] Text in L. G. Wickham Legg, *English Coronation Records* (Constable, London, 1901), pp.363-382.
[3] C. C. F. Greville, *A Journal of the Reign of Queen Victoria* (Longmans, Green & Co., London, 1887), vol. 1, pp.106f.

1820s and 1830s.[1] Even before Victoria's death scholarly publications related to coronations had begun to appear, and the number increased considerably after her demise, augmented of course by the flood of books and pamphlets of lesser quality. The more important editions of texts included Christopher Wordsworth, *The Manner of the Coronation of Charles the First of England*, Henry Bradshaw Society 2 (Harrison and Sons, London, 1892); Dr. John Wickham Legg, *Three Coronation Orders*, Henry Bradshaw Society 19 (Harrison and Sons, London, 1900); and his son, L. G. Wickham Legg, *English Coronation Records* (Constable, London, 1901). The general scholarly consensus was critical of what had been done to the rite in the seventeenth century and in favour of a return to the more ancient pattern.

However, long before the King's illness affected the matter, there was already pressure from both the King and others to abbreviate the service, raising fears among the scholars that this would lead to further mutilation. Thus those responsible for drawing up the rite had to seek to balance two quite different goals, although as it turned out, the two were not always in direct opposition to one another: sometimes a return to the older practice meant that lengthy later accretions could be omitted. Although Frederick Temple as Archbishop of Canterbury had ultimate responsibility for the form that the service was to take, it was Randall Davidson, then Bishop of Winchester, who had the greatest influence in the matter on the Coronation Committee appointed by the Privy Council, and his principal academic adviser was J. Armitage Robinson, then a Canon of Westminster but formerly Norrison Professor of Divinity at Cambridge University, a patristic scholar rather than a liturgiologist.[2]

Debate centred around two chief issues: what the bishops should wear on their heads and the details of the anointing. The former excited the greater popular concern. As yet, the wearing of mitres by bishops of the Church of England was still uncommon, and normal clerical headgear was a black cap. Robinson asserted that the earliest instance he could find of bishops putting on their caps during a coronation was in the rite for George I, and that it had 'probably come in by mere mistake, and I think that the Bishops ought not to do it. Their caps are simply their outdoor dress, and are forbidden by the Canons (I believe) to be worn in Church.'[3] However, Temple came under pressure from some to insist on the wearing of mitres, and under equal pressure from others to prevent that. The King was thought to favour mitres, and anglo-catholics got hold of an improbable story that silver mitres had been worn at the coronation of George II. On the other hand, some of the bishops wanted *purple* caps to be worn. In the end, Temple directed that all bishops were to *carry* square black velvet caps and wear rochets with sleeves; those officiating in any way were to wear copes, and all others the scarlet chimere (without hood) and black silk scarf.[4] Percy Dearmer had designed a new square cap, based on that worn by Archbishop Cranmer in the portrait in the National Portrait Gallery, and the canons of Westminster and a number of the bishops ordered them for the occasion.[5]

---

[1] Peter Hinchliff, 'Frederick Temple, Randall Davidson and the Coronation of Edward VII' in *Journal of Ecclesiastical History* 48 (1997), p.71.
[2] For further details, see *ibid.*, pp.79ff.
[3] *Ibid.*, p.83.
[4] *Ibid.*, pp.89-90.
[5] *Ibid.*, p.96.

The question of the anointing was rather more complicated. While Davidson wanted to restore the anointing of the breast and so return to the triple unction of head, breast, and hands[1] practised prior to the coronation of George IV, Temple himself thought it best that the head alone should be anointed: 'That and that alone is Biblical and the Biblical is best for Englishmen.'[2] Eventually, however, the King, almost certainly prompted by Davidson, expressed enthusiasm for the triple anointing, and it was restored to the rite.[3]

Nevertheless, there was a further dimension to the matter of the anointing. The suggestion was made from several quarters that the oil should be consecrated early in the morning on coronation day. Scholars believed that this was the ancient custom, and that ever since the Reformation it had been performed by a canon of Westminster who happened to be in episcopal orders. Peter Hinchliff has examined the basis for this belief and concluded that it 'seems to rest upon a series of misunderstandings and a modicum of wishful thinking'.[4] The rubrics of coronation rites from the late Middle Ages onwards require the oil to be placed on the altar early in the morning—but only among a great many other things that need to be got ready, and there is no mention of it being consecrated there. Hinchliff attributes the origin of the story of a canon of Westminster who was also a bishop consecrating it to Christopher Wordsworth's account of the coronation of Charles I, when William Laud, who was Subdean of the Abbey and also a bishop, had been asked by the King to take the role normally belonging to the Dean and apparently did consecrate the oil before the service. 'But later writers seem to have assumed that it was a regular feature of every coronation and to have gone on repeating the supposed "fact".' Hinchliff also goes on to point out that medieval English kings had been hallowed with what was said to be miraculous oil given to St. Thomas of Canterbury by the Blessed Virgin Mary—a story clearly intended to outdo the claim that the oil used for kings of France had been handed down from Clovis himself—and that this oil would therefore have been kept from one coronation to the next and would have needed no further consecration.[5] Be that as it may, scholars of the period thought that consecration earlier in the day was traditional, and so it was 'restored' on this occasion, being consecrated by Canon James Welldon, formerly Bishop of Calcutta.[6] Oil preserved from this coronation was used at that of George V[7]; and oil was again blessed semi-privately in St. Edward's Chapel prior to the coronations of George VI and the present Queen.

Other issues discussed in the course of preparing the rite included the question of who was to preach the sermon. It had been thought that the Bishop of London had a traditional right to be the preacher, but research revealed that only at the coronations of William IV and Victoria had this been the case, the occupant of the see on both occasions being C. J. Blomfield. Nevertheless, there seems to have been general agreement that the current Bishop of London, A. F. Winnington-Ingram, should be invited to preach.[8] It was also

---

[1] In that order—apparently not noticing that prior to 1689 the order had actually been hands, breast, and head.

[2] Hinchliff, 'Frederick Temple, Randall Davidson and the Coronation of Edward VII', pp.85-86.

[3] *Ibid.*, p.93.

[4] *Ibid.*, p.86.

[5] *Ibid.*, p.87.

[6] *Ibid.*, p.97-98. Hinchliff suggests that it was only added to the postponed service in order to 'relieve Temple from having to bless the oil during the service and to shorten the service itself', but since there never was a blessing prayer in the original printed order, this seems an unlikely explanation.

[7] Ratcliff, *The English Coronation Service*, p.45, n.2.

[8] Hinchliff, 'Frederick Temple, Randall Davidson and the Coronation of Edward VII', pp.88, 91.

decided that the Archbishop of York did not have an inherent right to perform the coronation of the Queen, but it was thought desirable that it should be someone other than the Archbishop of Canterbury. The King intimated that if Temple wished to invite someone else to crown the Queen, he would approve of its being the Archbishop of York (William Maclagan), and this was accepted.[1]

The rite finally produced was in general a great improvement on those of the preceding two centuries. It was shortened in a number of ways: it omitted the medieval First Oblation (when the sovereign offered a pall and a pound of gold in fulfillment of the commandment of Deut. 16.16: 'They shall not appear before the Lord empty-handed'), many of the Hanoverian anthems (including Handel's *Hallelujah Chorus*), the Ten Commandments, and the Proper Preface of the Communion Service; and the Litany and the address at the Presentation of the Bible were abridged. At the same time, some older features were restored: in addition to the triple unction, the wording of some of the forms of blessing of royal insignia was brought closer to earlier versions; an Introit to the Communion Service, 'O Hearken Thou . . .' (Ps. 5.2), was provided to replace the Sanctus which had long been improperly used for this purpose in English cathedrals; and a proper Collect was also provided for the Communion Service, based on a prayer in the tenth-century Pontifical of Egbert.

In the event, the postponement of the coronation because of the King's illness caused further changes being made in order to shorten it still more and reduce the strain on him. New orders of service were not printed, however, but the original ones were used, with manuscript alterations being made in the copies of the principal participants. The fourfold Recognition at the beginning, when the sovereign is presented to the people on each of the four sides of the 'Theatre' (as the raised platform erected between the sanctuary and the choir where the coronation takes place is designated), was reduced to a single form; the Litany was omitted completely; the sermon disappeared; and the *Te Deum* was moved from its position after the Benediction to the very end of the service, where it provided an appropriate concluding hymn of praise as the royal procession moved into St. Edward's Chapel. The last change has been retained at all other coronations during this century.

THE CORONATION OF GEORGE V

George V was crowned on 22 June 1911, with a rite only a little altered from that used for Edward VII.[2] At the crowning itself, a more ancient (and briefer) form of words was restored in place of the bombastic prose of Henry Compton's version drawn up for the coronation of William and Mary. The Introit to the Communion Service was changed to that which had been the Gradual chant in the medieval rite, 'Let my prayer come into thy presence as the incense . . .' (Ps. 141.2), and a Proper Preface was also restored. But the precedent of 1902, when the Archbishop of York crowned Queen Alexandra, was not followed, and Queen Mary was crowned by the Archbishop of Canterbury.

THE CORONATION OF GEORGE VI

At the coronation of George VI on 12 May 1937, several further changes were made.[3] First, the Litany was moved once more. In the medieval rite it had come immediately before the solemn anointing prayer, but at the coronation of James II it was transferred to a position before the sermon[4], and in 1689 it was placed at the beginning of the Communion

---

[1] *Ibid.*, p.91.
[2] Text in Ratcliff, *The English Coronation Service*, pp.71-106.
[3] Text, although with the excision of all the parts pertaining to the Queen, in Eeles, *The Coronation Service*, pp.63-84.
[4] This shift was apparently an afterthought by Archbishop Sancroft. who was responsible for revising the service: see H. A. Wilson, 'The English Coronation' in *Journal of Theological Studies* 2 (1901), p.499.

Service. Now, however, it was used to accompany the entrance procession of the Dean and canons of Westminster, where it also remained for the coronation of Elizabeth II. Obviously, the various revisers have had difficulty in seeing where it appropriately belongs. In ancient times at ordinations and other solemn blessings, the prayer of the presiding minister was always immediately preceded by a period of prayer by the congregation, often in the form of a litany, thus giving expression to the theological truth that liturgical and sacramental rites are the action of the whole Church, and not just of the ordained ministers. This seems to have been the function of the litany in the medieval coronation rite. Although its length would doubtless militate against its restoration to that position again, a special coronation litany might be substituted for it. This could perhaps be based on the series of short petitions, each with an 'Amen' response, in the coronation rite of the ancient 'Egbert' Pontifical, which were unfortunately welded together in later recensions into a single long prayer, *Benedic domine hunc regem*, and eventually omitted entirely in the excisions made for the coronation of James II.

Secondly, the Coronation Oath was moved from the position to which it had been transferred for the coronation of William and Mary. On that occasion, the whole coronation rite, with the exception of the entrance ceremonies and Recognition, had been moved and placed within the Communion Service, after the Creed. Because in the medieval structure the sermon and Oath (in that order) had followed the Recognition, this meant that the sermon now came in its usual position within the 1662 eucharistic rite, but the Oath was far removed from the Recognition to which it logically belongs: the sovereign takes the Oath in response to his/her election by the people. The 1937 rite, therefore, restored the connection by moving the Oath back to its earlier place. However, it also omitted the sermon entirely, and this omission was repeated at the coronation of Elizabeth II. Although shortening the long service a little, its disappearance is to be regretted. It is an ancient feature of the rite—from medieval times the rubric prescribed that one of the bishops should give a 'short and suitable' sermon—and is a vital component of a true ministry of the word.

Thirdly, at the anointing, the sequence followed prior to 1689 was restored, so that the hands were anointed first, then the breast, and finally the head.

THE CORONATION OF ELIZABETH II

Elizabeth's coronation, on 2 June 1953, brought with it some further changes from the order used for her father, nearly all of which improved its character.[1] Firstly, the connection between the Recognition and the Oath was further manifested by removing the procession of vessels and regalia, which had intervened between the two at the previous coronation, to the beginning of the rite, after the Queen's entrance. Secondly, the Presentation of the Bible, introduced at the coronation of William and Mary and located after the crowning, was moved to a position immediately following the Oath, since the Bible is not a part of the royal regalia. The wording of the accompanying address, which had been gradually shortened at successive coronations, was now lightly revised again, and the making of the presentation was entrusted to the Moderator of the General Assembly of the Church of Scotland—the first and so far only ecumenical gesture made in a coronation rite. Even in this position, however, the location of the presentation seems a little odd, since the Queen had already laid her hand upon the Bible in order to swear the Oath. In any case, following

---

[1] Text in E. C. Ratcliff, *The Coronation Service of Her Majesty Queen Elizabeth II* (SPCK, London/Cambridge University Press, 1953), pp.35-65.

previous custom, she did not keep it when she received it, but immediately returned it to the giver to place on the altar, which seems to weaken the symbolism of the act.

Thirdly, the Introit of the Communion Service was again changed to 'Behold, O God, our defender ...' (Ps. 84.9-10), being the original Introit of the medieval rite, with the previous version now being restored to its original medieval role as a Gradual; and a more faithful rendering of the Collect was substituted for that used at the previous three coronations.

Fourthly, at the investiture with the royal regalia, some apparent earlier confusion was now resolved. From medieval times the term 'Armills' (in the plural) had been applied to a single piece of silk worn like a stole around the sovereign's neck and tied to the elbows. (Later the singular 'Armill' was substituted, and from Queen Victoria's coronation onwards the ends were not tied but allowed to hang straight down.) But the word is derived from the Latin *armillae*, 'bracelets', and sovereigns wore bracelets at their coronation, even though these were not ritually presented to them. It would seem therefore that at some stage the delivery of the new stole-like garment replaced an earlier presentation of the bracelets, but the original name was still retained. Thus at Elizabeth's coronation the investing with the 'Armills' once again became a presentation of the bracelets, and the stole was now described as 'the Stole Royal'. Separate formulas for the delivery of the Armills, the Robe Royal with the Stole Royal, and the Orb also replaced the composite address which had been used since the coronation of William and Mary[1]; and the wording used at the delivery of other regalia, including the putting on of the Crown, and at the Benediction and Inthroning was revised, mainly so as to be more faithful to the older forms but occasionally to bring it more in line with contemporary realities.

Fifthly, at the Homage, the practice adopted at the coronation of Queen Victoria was revived: only Prince Philip kissed the Queen's cheek, and the rest kissed her right hand. Finally, the Communion service contained several innovations. At the offertory, a congregational hymn, 'All people that on earth do dwell', replaced the traditional anthem; after the offertory the Queen knelt at a faldstool before the altar instead of at her chair; and a prayer for, and blessing of, the Queen's Consort was introduced after the offertory and before the Prayer for the Church Militant. Not only was this last a complete innovation, but it was, rather strangely, not placed where the rite for the Queen was traditionally located at the coronation of a King—after the Homage and before the offertory. A new Proper Preface was provided; a communion anthem, omitted from the coronation of Charles II onwards, was restored; and after receiving communion, the Queen did not immediately return to her chair and resume the Crown, Sceptre, and Rod, as had been the previous practice, but remained at the faldstool until after Lord's Prayer and post-communion prayer had been said.

CONCLUSION

It seems clear that the chief architect of the revision of the rite made for the coronation of Elizabeth II was the liturgical scholar Edward Ratcliff, Ely Professor of Divinity at Cambridge, especially since most of the changes reflect criticisms that he had put forward at the time of the coronation of George VI.[2] His principal aim appears to have been the

---

[1] The separate formula for the Armills was revived at the coronation of George I, but fell into disuse again from the coronation of William IV onwards.

[2] See Ratcliff, *The English Coronation Service*.

restoration, wherever possible, of elements from the medieval rite, and the removal of much of the language and many of the features introduced at the coronations of James II and of William and Mary, which twentieth-century scholars had universally condemned as destructive. In that respect, he was largely continuing the work begun at the coronation of Edward VII. In general, Ratcliff's work can only be applauded, particularly when one recalls how very conservative was the liturgical and cultural climate of 1953. But it is not incapable of further improvement, especially in the light of the changed world of today—both culturally and liturgically. I have already set out in some detail elsewhere my criticism of the 1953 rite[1], and will not repeat it here, except to list the principal areas that I believe demand attention in any future revision.

(a) Ecumenical and possibly interfaith participation. The inclusion of the Moderator of the General Assembly of the Church of Scotland was a step in the right direction, but only a step. According to Randolph Churchill, the possible participation of 'the Free Churches, and the Moslems and Hindus, who are part of the Commonwealth' was considered in 1953, but was not acted upon.[2] In today's climate, this issue cannot, and should not, be avoided.

(b) The wording of the Coronation Oath as regards the claims made for the Church of England. Although any action in this regard would require an Act of Parliament, it should not be impossible to find a way for the Oath to continue to affirm a positive role for the Church of England within the nation, without sounding so exclusive of other churches and faiths.

(c) The eucharistic context. Anglican eucharistic rites and practice have changed much in the last forty-five years, and this should be reflected in the coronation rite. A much fuller ministry of the word, including an Old Testament reading, is now more normal in Anglican services, and the omission of the traditional short sermon at the last few coronations cannot really be defended. If it is desired to abbreviate the service, there are better ways of doing that.[3] The retention of an 'offertory prayer' in the coronation rite is a nice piece of antiquarianism, but out of line with current trends in eucharistic revision. And the absence of any opportunity for the reception of Holy Communion by the wider congregation would also be unusual in modern eucharistic practice.

(d) Congregational participation. In 1953, apart from the acclamations by the people at the Recognition at the beginning and again after the Homage, the rest of the service had the appearance of a rite performed by the clergy at which the congregation were mere spectators. The only concession made to congregational participation at this time was the introduction of the hymn, 'All people that on earth do dwell'. One of the fruits of the twentieth-century liturgical movement is that the congregation now plays a far more active part in liturgical worship than did Christians of earlier generations. Thus it would be desirable not only to include more congregational singing, but to restore to the rite provision for congregational prayer for the sovereign—the true role of the litany, which earlier revisers have apparently failed to recognize as they desperately moved it around the service trying to find a suitable home for it.

(e) The anointing. This central action symbolizes on the one hand the divine sanction for the choice of particular individual and the promise of the outpouring of God's grace in the task which lies ahead, and on the other hand the new king or queen's solemn and

---

[1] Paul F. Bradshaw, 'On Revising the Coronation Service' in *Theology* 96 (1993), pp.300-307.
[2] Randolph Churchill, *The Story of the Coronation* (verschoyle, London, 1953), p.87.
[3] For example, the Homage might be entirely removed from the service and done elsewhere later in the day, since it is not an integral part of the rite.

lifelong commitment to faithful service in the office which has been entrusted to him/ her. It is a pity that Temple's preference at the coronation of Edward VII for returning to the most ancient—and Old Testament—practice of anointing the head alone was not followed, for that would make its symbolic significance clearer, as would a return to the older tradition of the sovereign kneeling to receive it: kings and queens have sat down for this part of the service only since the coronation of Charles I in 1626. While this more recent custom clearly emphasizes the divine legitimation of the monarch, it is less expressive of the humble petition for the gift of divine grace so that the recipient 'may be enabled to the discharge of his/her weighty office' (as the offertory prayer at the eucharist puts it). Finally, the anointing prayer itself needs to be rewritten. In its present form it dates only from 1689 (with some subsequent amendments), when most of the rich language of the earlier version was lost and it was transformed almost entirely into a petition for the outpouring of the sevenfold gifts on the Holy Spirit on the sovereign, borrowed from the confirmation service of the Book of Common Prayer. Such a rewriting will also involve making a decision as to whether the oil is to be consecrated beforehand or during this prayer, or whether the sovereign alone and not the material element is to be blessed.

Appendix to Chapter 2

THE STRUCTURE OF THE CORONATION RITE IN 1953

The diagrammatic outline of the 1953 structure shown on the facing pages 32 and 33 overleaf is drawn from the text published in E. C. Ratcliff, *The Communion Service of Her Majesty Queen Elizabeth II.*

I   THE PREPARATION [The litany is sung during preliminary processions]
II   THE ENTRANCE INTO THE CHURCH
        The Queen enters and is received with an Anthem from Psalm 122, prays quietly, and
        goes to her Chair; Lords carrying Regalia present them to the Archbishop, who passes
        them to the Dean of Westminster who lays them on the Altar
III   THE RECOGNITION
        The Archbishop 'presents' the Queen to four compass points, and the people shout 'GOD
        SAVE QUEEN ELIZABETH'
IV   THE OATH
        The Queen takes the Coronation Oath, to govern justly, to 'maintain in the United
        Kingdom the Protestant Reformed Religion established by law', and to uphold the Church
        of England
V   THE PRESENTING OF THE HOLY BIBLE
        The Moderator of the Church of Scotland presents to the Queen the Bible 'the most
        valuable thing that this world affords'
VI   THE BEGINNING OF THE COMMUNION SERVICE
        [All texts are 1662 unless stated otherwise]
        The Introit (Psalm 84.9-10)
        The Collect for Purity
        The Collect for the Queen [unique to Coronation rites]
        The Epistle (1 Peter 2.13-17)
        The Gradual (Psalm 141.2)
        The Gospel (Matthew 22.15-22)
        The Nicene Creed (sung)
VII   THE ANOINTING
        'Come Holy Ghost'
        Prayer over the Ampulla of oil
        Anthem 'Zadok the priest' (The Queen moves to King Edward's Chair)
        The Archbishop anoints the Queen's palms, breast, and head, and prays that she
            'be anointed, blessed and consecrated Queen over the People'
        Blessing of the Queen for the task of monarchy
VIII   THE PRESENTING OF THE SPURS AND SWORD, AND THE OBLATION
        OF THE SAID SWORD
        The spurs are presented
        The sword is presented, and prayer said for the execution of justice
        The Queen returns it to the altar (whence a peer 'redeems' it and then carries it)
XI   THE INVESTING WITH THE ARMILLS, THE STOLE ROYAL AND THE
        ROBE ROYAL: AND THE DELIVERY OF THE ORB
        The Armills [Bracelets] are put on the Queen's wrists with injunctions
        The Robe and Stole are put on the Queen (now standing) with injunctions
        The Delivery of the Orb with injunctions ['this Orb set under the Cross']
X   THE INVESTITURE PER ANNULUM, ET PER SCEPTRUM ET BACULUM
        The Ring, Sceptre and Rod are delivered to the Queen with injunctions
XI   THE PUTTING ON OF THE CROWN
        The Archbishop says a blessing of Crown and of Queen
        The Archbishop crowns the Queen
        The people shout 'GOD SAVE THE QUEEN'
        The Princes, Princesses etc. put on coronets etc. Trumpets sound, guns at Tower fire
        The Archbishop prays that God may crown the Queen with a crown of glory
        Anthem 'Be strong and of good courage'

XII   THE BENEDICTION
Series of blessings of the Queen ['faithful Parliaments and quiet realms']

XIII THE INTHRONING
The Queen is lifted into the Throne by Bishops and Peers
The Archbishop enjoins her to 'hold fast' and prays that God may establish her Throne

XIV THE HOMAGE
The Archbishops and Bishops pay homage
The Duker of Edinburgh pays homage ['become your liege man']
Dukes, Peers etc. pay homage
Anthems accompany homage ('Rejoice in the Lord alway', 'O clap your hands', 'I will
   not leave you comfortless', 'O Lord our Governour: how excellent', 'Thou wilt keep
   him in perfect peace')
Drums and Trumpets lead into shout
   GOD SAVE QUEEN ELIZABETH
   LONG LIVE QUEEN ELIZABETH
   MAY THE QUEEN LIVE FOR EVER

XV   THE COMMUNION
Hymn 'All people that on earth do dwell'
The Queen takes off her crown and goes to steps of altar
The Queen offers bread and wine for communion
The Archbishop prays for the sanctification of the gifts and fruitfulness for the   Queen
The Queen offers gifts of a cloth and of a pound of gold
The Duke of Edinburgh kneels beside her at faldstools
The Archbishop prays for the Duke and gives him a blessing
The Prayer for the Church Militant here in Earth
The Invitation
The General Confession
The Absolution and Comfortable Words
Sursum Corda
The Prayer of Humble Access
The Prayer of Consecration
The Communion of: The two Archbishops, The Dean of Westminster, The two
   Bishops Assistant, The Queen and the Duke of Edinburgh
Anthem 'O taste, and see'
The Lord's Prayer
The Prayer of Oblation
The Queen resumes her Crown and returns to her Throne
Gloria in Excelsis
The Archbishop prays 'Prevent us, O Lord . . .' and the blessing 'The peace   of God'

XVI TE DEUM LAUDAMUS
The choir sings Te Deum

XVII THE RECESS
Processions out, with appropriate divesting
THE NATIONAL ANTHEM

3. The Next Coronation

by
COLIN BUCHANAN

(A) THE OCCASION

Once upon a time, over twenty years ago as I write, Ronald Jasper, the then chairman of the Liturgical Commission, came into a meeting of the Commission a little late and apologized thus: 'I am sorry to be late, but I have just been arranging the Queen's funeral'. We, the ordinary members of the Commission, asked—and learned—of him whether or not it would be antique in its language—and elaborate in its trimmings. Common sense decrees that such a programme should be in waiting (like *The Times*' obituaries) during the lifetime of their subject. Not only would the monarch herself presumably have firm views as to the contents of such a service, but, when the time came that the service would be actually needed, it would have to be put into operation with a high degree of administrative perfection in a matter of a very few days, days moreover in which not only was the person most chiefly concerned dead, but most other people concerned were in a state of advanced shock.

The next coronation, though precipitated by the same not-to-be-wished-for decease, does not suffer from quite the same timetable handicaps, for there would presumably be rather more time available for planning the event after the present monarch had died. However, there is a comparison involved at the moment, for it is well worth noting that there are clearly considerable difficulties for the most obviously 'interested parties' in giving their minds to the issue, or in so consulting as to be putting ideas on paper, whilst the present monarch is alive and literally present. Indeed, to be ruthlessly accurate, we do not even know for sure who the 'interested parties' are—for, quite apart from speculation about the logical possibility of the present Heir Apparent waiving his right of succession, or actually abdicating after inheriting, none can be sure that his mother will in fact predecease him; and there is precedent in the British Royal Family for a grandson inheriting the throne (which happened in 1760), and elsewhere, as, e.g., in France in 1715, for a great-grandson doing so.

So we return to the interval from succession to coronation. On 2 June 1953 there had been fifteen months from the death of George VI to the coronation of the present Queen, and that sounds like a more plausible time-scale. Equally the new monarch was herself available (as was her consort), with whom the Archbishop of Canterbury could negotiate sensitive or indeterminate matters. On the other hand, Carpenter's biography of Geoffrey Fisher makes it clear that the fifteen months were not really sufficient in that case, and it is at least arguable that Archbishop Fisher did not face anything like as difficult a set of problems as those which would confront Archbishop Carey in the event of the present Queen's decease.[1] I have written elsewhere that none must pray for her health more

---

[1] Edward Carpenter, *Archbishop Fisher—His Life and Times* (Canterbury Press, Norwich, 1991) pp.245-267.

fervently than the Archbishop does[1]; and it has to be confessed in respect of our present Queen that both the longevity of her mother on the one hand and the apparent resilience and energy with which she herself still goes about her tasks in her eighth decade on the other, suggest that, with or without such supportive prayer from the Archbishop, she may well live far past his retirement date. *Caveat successor eius*. But, in the economy of God, it is sensible to think that the day may come *some* time; and, if this is so, then some advance thinking by liturgists is not only prudent, but might possibly also be a rare and welcome chance to stretch their own creative talents. Such an event currently appears to come about as frequently as Halley's Comet—or even Hale-Bopp—but (unlike either of these two comets) it looks bound to appear above the horizon some time fairly soon—or even very soon.[2]

(B) PLANNING RESPONSIBILITIES—THE ROLE OF THE ARCHBISHOP OF CANTERBURY

It appears that in 1952, immediately on the death of George VI, there met a 'Coronation Commission' (the membership of which—notably the Duke of Edinburgh and the Earl Marshal—must have already been established and is presumably (like a Church of England Vacancy in See Committee) always in being, ready to act if occasion requires). The part of such a Commission is to plan and implement the whole set of ceremonies from setting up stands along the Mall and granting permission to use the royal insignia on commemoration mugs to ensuring the right police protection for visiting Heads of State. In 1952 soon after the King's death the Privy Council followed this by appointing its own 'Coronation Committee', and this Committee, which largely acted through its Executive, resolved in full Committee on 16 June 1952 that the Archbishop of Canterbury 'inspect the Office of Divine Service to be used on the day of Her Majesty's Coronation in the Abbey of Westminster and that his Grace do, in obedience to the commands of Her Majesty, consider in what respect it may be proper consistently with the due solemnity of the occasion to abridge the said Service and present the same to the Committee.'[3] The Coronation Committee was thus taking a specific responsibility for the particular liturgical event in the Abbey. It looks from the form of the resolution as though the rightness of the Abbey for the event was taken for granted (it is *the* historic place, and is *the* London 'Royal Peculiar', and it contains King Edward's Chair, and at that time it also contained the Stone of Scone). On the other hand, it is just possible that the role of the Archbishop was not quite being taken for granted, and had at least to be the subject of a resolution rather than the invoking of a known standing order or an unbreakable historic convention. And the instruction to the Archbishop in respect of the rite was clearly of a much more contingent sort, in that he was being asked to 'abridge' the orders available to him from history. This would suggest that the form of the liturgy lies in the discretion of any group appointed by the Privy Council following the death of the present monarch. Nothing from the past (save perhaps the Abbey and the Chair—and a Crown) can be assumed to be beyond review. However, between the lines, we must reckon a powerful, if invisible, role would be assumed by the

---

[1] See my *Cut the Connection: The Church of England and Disestablishment* (DLT, 1994), p.146

[2] I begin to suspect that the present Queen has become such an enduring landmark in Britain that imaginations cannot easily stretch to what life would be like without her. But her decease is subject to much the same considerations of providence as are others', and it is helpful to grappling with the contingencies of this essay to contemplate her death as fully possible whilst the present Study is at the press, or in the brief period remaining before the next millennium, as well as mentally postponing it another twenty years or more.

[3] Clive Mansell in an unpublished letter of 10 October 1994 based on his researches on a Windsor mid-term Course.

new monarch himself or herself. Nor is it likely that anyone other than the Archbishop of Canterbury would be given responsibility for compiling the initial draft of the liturgy. Clive Mansell writes (in relation to 1952) as follows:

'Whilst the Archbishop was the recipient of a resolution that he should set up the Coronation liturgy, it could very properly be argued that the right to be responsible for the liturgy was first and foremost his and that it could not be devolved elsewhere, unless he declined it. The whole area of the Coronation is surrounded by legal matters and a Court of Claims is set up when a Coronation is pending to resolve such issues. This could be a matter of importance at some future stage, especially if there are attempts to require the liturgy to be drawn up by an inter-faith Council. It seems to me that a future Archbishop will need to hold on to his rights of office in this matter, whilst wisely choosing to consult whom he will . . .'[1]

If of course the Church of England were disestablished (on which I write more below), it is by no means clear that the Archbishop of Canterbury would have any 'rights' to direct the character of the ceremonial. But severing the Church of England from the State would certainly take time, and (granted the present reluctance of Church leaders to pursue it) it would probably take more time than is available before the next coronation is due. The situation would of course be oddly complicated if the process of disestablishing were under way or *sub judice* at the time the present monarch died. But the broad assumption must be that the Archbishop of Canterbury of the day would receive instructions for providing the liturgy. As before, such an Archbishop would be free to call in all sorts of liturgical expertise (in line with Paul Bradshaw's identification in the previous essay of the role played in 1952 by Edward Ratcliff[2]). And these essays are themselves constructed with a view to being of assistance to that Archbishop (be he—or she—the present incumbent of Lambeth or another archiepiscopal unknown arising further on in the next millennium) in that highly demanding role.

The 1952 Coronation Committee and Archbishop Geoffrey Fisher had various historically conditioned questions to resolve about the rite. These included the still famous ones about the possible inclusion of the Duke of Windsor and the (also controversial) issue about possible permission for the TV cameras to broadcast the service. It is a matter of history that they said 'no' to the former and 'yes' to the latter.[3] On the other hand they were not faced with the variety of difficult issues any future such Committee will have to handle, some of which are outlined by Paul Bradshaw in the previous essay.

The different strands of these relevant question-posing issues with which such future liturgists will have to engage would appear at this point in time to include in broad terms the following: the realities of the current church-state relationship, the Christian liturgical frame within which those relationships are to be expressed, certain ecumenical questions, and, to some as yet undefined extent, the personal beliefs and aspirations of the new monarch who is at the heart of the rite.

(C) CHURCH AND STATE

At the moment the Church of England remains the 'established' Church of the land, a kind of semi-independent semi-chained department of state.[4] Just as the government of

---

[1] Clive Mansell in his unpublished Windsor dissertation.
[2] See P. Bradshaw in chapter 2 above, pp.29-30.
[3] These are not mentioned by Bradshaw.
[4] For a fuller description of the present Church-State links see my book, *Cut the Connection: op.cit.* chs.4-7.

the day is 'Her Majesty's Government' so, in the last analysis, is the Church of England 'Her Majesty's Church'. But the departmental chains are in our case not very confining, and most of the time are not even obvious. The sense of ecclesiastical independence in the Church of England is strong and it corresponds to the sheer facts of the present establishment position. But the chains are nevertheless there—and the great point about them, the reason why we do not daily sense them, is that, although they are not weak, they are *long*. A captive on a long chain can walk within the limit of his long chain for much of the day or much of the year—and he only really discovers the binding and unbreakable character of the chains when he comes to the very limit of them, and finds himself then brought up short. So it has been when, for instance, the House of Commons turned down two Church of England Measures in the 1980s, or took twelve months, after much buffetting by the Ecclesiastical Committee of Parliament, to handle the ordination of women in 1993, that the Church of England has really learned that, despite that sense of freedom which a sufficiently long chain deceitfully conveys, it really is a chain, and we really are held captive by it.

The same sense of being captive is, of course, also conveyed in the method of the appointment of bishops, and particularly of diocesan bishops. Here the process includes the agreed convention that the Crown Appointments Commission should forward two names to the Prime Minister for him (or her, as it was for eleven years) to choose between those two, with absolute discretion to prefer the one less favoured by the Commission. Indeed the existing convention allows for the Prime Minister of the day to send both names back to the Church of England and ask for two more, though it is likely that this power has never been invoked in the twenty years since the Crown Appointments Commission first began work.[1] Here again the Church of England suddenly at intervals finds itself at the limit of its chain—and arguably it does so every time the appointment of a new bishop is announced not from Lambeth or York, not from General Synod, not from the vacant diocese, but *from Downing Street.*

It is when Downing Street has made the offer, and received the assent of the chosen candidate and has then forwarded the chosen name to the Palace, that the name is released to the media. There then follows the dreadful *congé d'élire*, in which the Dean (or Provost) and Chapter of the cathedral of the vacant diocese are required under Henry VIII's legislation of 1534, still current, to vote for Her Majesty's nominee—the sole candidate, who is a royal nominee, whose name has already been released to the press. The Dean and Chapter having duly and obediently (as is required of subjects) done their bit, the name of the elected person is sent to the Provincial Registrar for a totally arcane ceremony of 'confirmation'. This requires the person appearing before those conducting the ceremony to demonstrate he is the man elected by the Dean and Chapter. When he has done this, he is actually 'confirmed', and thus becomes legally the bishop of the vacant diocese—even if he is not yet consecrated as a bishop in the Church of God. In this latter event he will be consecrated the next day. Consecration of a bishop is effected through the monarch providing a mandate to the Archbishop of the Province requiring him to consecrate. The Archbishop can only act on the instruction. Finally the newly elected, confirmed and consecrated bishop attends the monarch to pay homage, in the course of which he has to take

---

[1] At the delayed point of finally going to press, in mid-September 1997, the media are full of rumours that the new Prime Minister, Tony Blair, has declined both names submitted by the Crown Appointments Commission for the diocese of Liverpool, and has asked for more. There appears to be some substance to the rumours, and that appears to be conceded by Downing Street.

the famous (and until recently secret) oath:

I . . .

lately . . .

having been elected, confirmed and consecrated Bishop of...

do hereby declare

that your Majesty is the only Supreme Governor of this your realm

in spiritual and ecclesiastical things

as well as temporal

and no foreign prelate or potentate

has any jurisdiction within this realm

and I acknowledge that I hold the said bishopric

as well the spiritualities as the temporalities thereof

only of your Majesty

and for the same temporalities I do my homage presently to your Majesty

so help me God

God save Queen Elizabeth[1]

After paying homage, a new diocesan may be safely enthroned, and he is now secure. But he—and his diocese—have briefly experienced the imprisoning chain. The monarch is governor—or 'protector'—of the Church of England. The implications are far-reaching, and the more so because we are a constitutional monarchy in which the absolute powers of the monarch are largely exercised through the Prime Minister of the day.[2] The way in which these powers over the Church have been enshrined in the Coronation liturgy are outlined in chapter 2 above.[3]

There remains a question about the reality of the relationship envisaged. The concept that the Queen 'rules' over her 'subjects' has been precious to the English (and the British) people, and, however dated it may be, it is likely that a large proportion of the citizens of Britain and Northern Ireland are content enough with that nomenclature. Republicanism, whilst visibly on the increase and actually approaching the threshhold of general visibility, is still the persuasion of only a tiny splinter group of the total populace. We may therefore reasonably safely anticipate that there will be a coronation after the Queen's death, and that a great issue needing addressing is the degree of establishment of the Church of England likely to be prevailing at the time of the event, rather than whether there should be any succeeding monarch at all. (This latter hypothesis, if taken seriously, would of course trump all the ceremonial aces, and bring discussion of coronations to an abrupt end at this point.)

The actual form of the question in 1953 ran as follows:

Archbishop: Will you to the utmost of your power maintain the Laws of God and the true profession of the Gospel? Will you to the utmost of your power maintain in the United Kingdom the Protestant Reformed Religion established by law? Will you maintain and preserve inviolably the settlement of the Church of England, and the doctrine, worship, discipline and government thereof, as by law established in England? And will you preserve unto the Bishops and Clergy of England, and to the

---

[1] This was never freely published until *Cut the Connection* came out (see pages 83-84 in it); and I had earlier asked a question in General Synod and been told by the Secretary-General that the text was not his to release. It has been no part of the Prime Minister's invitation to his preferred candidate to inform him of the Oath, and so the bishop designate has necessarily gleaned it at some later stage when all decisions are already made. It was officially denied in Synod by the then Clerk of the Closet that new bishops have not known what the Oath contained until they came to swear it. This was however still the case in the mid-1980s!

[2] This is discussed more fully in *Cut the Connection*.

[3] See Bradshaw, p.25 above.

Churches there committed to their charge, all such rights and privileges, as by law do or shall appertain to them or any of them?

However, a major presupposition of the traditional coronation appears to lie not so much in the 'establishment' area of the particularities of the monarch's relationship to bishops or synods of the Church of England, but rather in the area of the quasi-sacramental Christian anointing of the monarch as the symbol and means of God's both earmarking and equipping for the task of monarchy. That sounds right in a Christian nation; but the nature of the nation is part of the very matter at issue; and in an era when the monarchy provides the Head of State for various nations in the Commonwealth, let alone an era when, even within England, the nation of England is in no way numerically coterminous with the Church of England, the traditional coronation liturgy involves an assertion that the God and Father of Jesus Christ is the true God, that this God has called this monarch to this responsibility, and that this anointing is with a view to the whole of the monarchical task, and not simply to that of being Supreme Governor of the Church of England. The Old Testament citations (memorably enshrined in 1953 in the music of 'Zadok the priest'!) to that extent cover up an ambiguity or a dual role; for the Davidic kings were intended by God to be protectors of the whole religious life of the whole nation, and were responsible for ensuring a unity of religious and social life embracing all the people of Israel in all areas of their tribal, social and personal lives. By contrast to-morrow's monarch has almost by definition to be viewing the whole of the task as one sort of God-given role, and the Supreme Governor's role as quite another. It is a very odd upshot.

Disestablishment, if it were accomplished prior to the succession occurring, would presumably draw all the distinctively 'C/E' features away from the coronation. The monarch, if a convinced Christian, might well include an act of Christian worship somewhere within the rituals—and, through the current location of King Edward's Chair (as well as sentiment), might even do so inside Westminster Abbey. But it would be impossible for the compiler of the ceremonies to build in the Old Testament Davidic concepts set out above; it would be impossible to ask the monarch to swear oaths on behalf of the Church of England; and it would be quite erroneous to include reference to 'the Protestant Reformed Religion established by law'. All this might, of course, make it easier to run an ecumenical type of service.

So much for the 'Christian but disestablished' scenario. In fact we may encounter as the more likely situation the current 'not very Christian, but still established'. It is that which we have to address. In particular, we address it on the assumption that its context is the succession to the Crown of the present Heir Apparent. And it should be noted that, despite all sorts of correspondence and public assertions, the monarch's oath to uphold the Church of England has no force if Parliament produces a Measure or an Act to disestablish it. The monarch is bound to give to all Parliamentary enactments whatsoever the formal Royal Assent, and this happened when Queen Victoria in 1869, having promised at her coronation to uphold 'the United Church of England and Ireland', nevertheless let the Church of Ireland go when the Act for disestablishing it came before her, and the title of the established church in England was consequently changed. Similarly George V let the Welsh dioceses lapse from the Church of England, despite *his* Coronation Oath. If a monarch were to deem such an Assent as in breach of his or her original Coronation Oath in such a way that in conscience he or she would have to withhold the Assent, then a constitutional crisis of a totally insoluble sort would ensue. The constitutional monarchy would be unravelling over a relatively minor issue. No monarch could really hold such a conscience, and it is a matter for relief that the precedents mentioned here run wholly in the other direction.[1]

---

[1] See *Cut the Connection*, pp.148-9.

(D) THE LITURGICAL TEXT

Prince Charles has emerged strongly in public in recent years as a patron of the Prayer Book Society, and has forcefully stated not only that the ancient 1662 text is our true and rich inheritance, but also that modern texts are a mess of pottage. He has not always appeared well briefed in his utterances, notably in a recent one where he stated that Cranmer's work, when it was written, represented stability and continuity in a time of turbulence. But his predilections appear very clearly.

Before, however, we assume that a coronation must be conducted in Tudor language, we should note certain wedges in favour of modern language which are being driven into any historical conservatism of either the Prince or the previous coronation rites:

(a) Firstly (and often forgotten), the Prince himself, when he married Diana in 1981, had the marriage itself in Prayer Book English, but the prayers in a contemporary style;

(b) Other great public occasions, whether Remembrance Sunday in many borough or civic situations or the enthronement of bishops, have similarly moved over; and the Prince himself was present in May 1997 at Canterbury cathedral where the service to commemorate the fourteen hundred years since the coming of Augustine was comparably 'mod'.

There have been mavericks amongst our leaders, and, for instance, the present Bishop of London, alleged to be a friend of the Prince, was himself consecrated at his own request with the BCP Ordinal. But such museum-piece uses are rare. Is a future coronation to be such a consciously ancient liturgical museum-piece? This would of course affect not only the choice of eucharistic rite, but also the language used for the specific coronation rituals.

The ministry of the word as previously used actually lacked the very royalist elements we might have expected. Being a 1662 communion, the rite had no Old Testament reading, so the chance to magnify the role of King David was missed; and the readings of 1 Peter 2.13-15 and Matthew 22.15-22 look more like texts for Christians living under an alien monarchy than for super-royalist ones. Then Paul Bradshaw in the last essay, puts up a plea for the restoration of a sermon.[1] Certainly there are instances of great royal events (such as the present queen's marriage and also her coronation) without a sermon; but, if this is to be a truly eucharistic event, it will be sadly lacking if there is to be a truncated sermonless ministry of the word.

Presumably most of the special ceremonies would then follow the ministry of the word—notably the anointing, the delivery of spurs, sword, armills, vestments, orb, ring, sceptre, rod, glove, and then the crowning, enthroning and homage.[2] They might or might not be pruned, and there would be a question about the place of intercessions (for the 'Church Militant' prayer in 1662 is placed after the setting of the Communion Table, but that would not work in modern rites). If a modern eucharistic liturgy is used, there might also then be a question about sharing the Peace, though it is acknowledged that the present monarch, when at a major communion service, is already usually kept separated from this somewhat egalitarian procedure. The existing curious 'offertory' prayer would have to go, though it is to be hoped that the Roman ones would not come in its place.[3]

---

[1] See above p.30.

[2] It is doubtful whether most of these are integral to a *Christian* ceremony at all—the anointing being the most plausibly treated as quasi-sacramental—and it is arguable that the actual arraying has to be considered afresh with each coronation that comes, and it is not strictly Christian liturgical considerations which expand or reduce the list.

[3] An oblation of the elements at this point (such as the stark English rendering of the Roman prayers evinces) is no improvement on the extraordinary epiclesis upon them, unique to coronations thus far.

(E) AN ECUMENICAL EVENT?

A different kind of new situation arises from a changed ecumenical context. In 1937 there was no distinguishable non-Anglican participation; but in 1953 the then Moderator of the Church of Scotland got a small look-in by presenting the Bible—one of the preliminaries prior to the beginning of the communion service. The wording of this included no mention of Scotland, and the Moderator, despite his prominent if brief appearance, was not thereby being invited to receive communion. But the history of the crown makes it very clear that the same monarch who is supreme governor of the Church of England by dint of being Queen of England is also the most highly respected member of Church of Scotland by dint of being Queen of Scotland, and the present monarch manifests that membership whenever in Scotland. The participation of the Moderator from that point of view was making no concession to ecumenism in England, nor, for what it was worth, in Scotland. Despite English loose talk, the Church of Scotland would not normally call itself a 'Free Church', but conceives of itself rather as 'the national Church'.

The dilemma about other denominations starts to emerge. If the leaders of the other Christian denominations or of the present 'ecumenical instruments' (the multi-nation Council of Churches of Britain and Ireland and the four separate national instruments) are to take a public part, they clearly cannot stand level with the Church of England at the event which enthrones the Supreme Governor of the Church of England and textually expresses that governorship and special relationship in fairly strong terms; on the other hand at a Christian service it seems reasonable to expect that Christian Churches ought to have a different place from representatives of other faiths. In other words, if the Church of England is established on anything like the present terms, the rite must by definition give that Church pre-eminence (though it would certainly be possible for leaders of other denominations to read the scriptures, to present one or two of the regalia, to lead intercessions, to assist with the distribution of communion, and even, if we are allowed to dream, to preach). It must, I take it, be recognizably a Church of England rite in terms of personnel, texts, milieu and style, even if there are guest appearances within it of other Christians. If it were truly ecumenical it would cease to recognize or confer a specially protected and privileged place in the nation for the Church of England. That might be viewed as good or ill, but what it is not is 'established'. The dilemma of privilege and the ambiguity of captivity are both bound to be focussed in the coronation rite.

The position of other faith communities is different again. There is plenty of precedent for their taking part in giving a welcome to, say, a new vicar or other ecclesiastical person in the context of a communion service; and that kind of involvement would be appropriate within the paying of Homage or some extension of it.[1] It is only a short step from there to think in terms rather of national communities and to look for stages of welcome (with the appropriate degree of submission or homage or peer-greeting) from representatives of the dominions, of other Commonwealth nations, and of other foreign nations

---

[1] We often speak or write as though we know who the 'other faith-communities' are—and certainly there are world religions in good standing in Britain, such as Islam and Judaism. But the concept, however charitable in its intention, should not be viewed as indiscriminately all-embracing, and I have become accustomed in my own pastoral ministry to viewing the socially nearest 'other faith-communities' as frequently being Freemasonry, Spiritualism and Satanism, and it is not at all clear that these can be viewed by Christians as 'in good standing', or can easily be swept into any positive attitude we may wish to take towards 'other faiths'. I make this point without prejudice to the general standing of the major 'world faiths'.

Finally, there is the question of the distribution of communion. The 1953 rite, using the BCP communion text, had that long-standing internal contradiction, that there was first an invitation to communion read to the whole Abbeyful:

'Ye that do truly and earnestly repent..., and are in love and charity . . . and intend to lead a new life...Draw near with faith, and take this holy Sacrament . . .'

This, however, was followed by detailed rubrics making it clear that no more than seven persons in all were actually going to be communicated. It is at least arguable that, if there is to be a Christian eucharist, then Christians from all round the world ought to have a chance to share with their monarch in the sacrament. If that simultaneously exposes large numbers of non-communicants, then that is a paradox consequential upon the curious establishment of a minority religion within this country. A protected privileged communion of certain interested parties is a relic of a distorted individualism in relation to the sacrament—the lesser of two evils is an 'open' communion rite which, having invited all, then discovers that the 'great and the good' of the land are not all Christian communicants.

(E) THE MONARCH'S PERSONAL POSITION

If we are to assume both an established Church of England and the succession of the present Heir Apparent, then certain more personal questions arise around his own person, In essence these are matters firstly of faith and secondly of morals.

The Prince of Wales, at his most injudicious, has been heard both to equate all religions and to say he wished to be 'Defender of Faith' rather than 'Defender of the Faith'.[1] He is thought to have meant by this that he wanted to be seen as somehow symbolically 'for' all faiths; for on inspection he would not have any special *powers* in relation to them (it is up to the Parliaments in sovereign nations truly to 'defend' particular faiths—or not.). It might well, however, be argued that, when all are thus defended, none are; and it might also be difficult to distinguish between the monarch's 'defence' of (respectively) Christianity, Islam, New Age, Ba'Hai, and Satanism. It looks at the time of writing as though someone has taken him aside and pointed out the impracticability of his implied programme, and has even suggested that it would be politic, if he is to inherit the role of Supreme Governor of the Church of England, if he at least showed some esteem for that institution. There have, at the time of writing, been some hints that he wishes to act on that suggestion.

Alongside this, there has also been a question as to whether he is an actual communicant. It would be odd if he were to be receiving communion at his coronation with no history of doing so in the preceding years, let alone with no intention of doing so again. Again there have been some official leaks to indicate that he is a communicant, though Anglicans at large had not suspected it. The coronation later requires him to be.[2]

It must be added that one of the concealed unfairnesses of the establishment is that the monarch is forced into a visible and communicant Anglican role. When the whole of the rest of the country has been given permission lawfully to slip away from the imposed Anglicanism of the Tudor regime, the monarchs themselves have not. They alone must

---

[1] Paradoxically, it has always struck me that the Latin original might well be translated as 'Defender of Faith', but I have not heard the Prince claim that his meaning was there all along...

[2] There is, of course, precedent for a monarch declining to communicate—the very position of the papist King James II in 1685 (see chapter 1 above). For an incoming monarch to declare that receiving communion was beyond his expectations or intentions would sound very much as though he were dropping the Church of England from his responsibilities.

believe to order, believe in this way to order, act in accord with this belief to order, and stay that way for life. The unexamined assumptions here are frightening for the liberty of the individual; and the tension must be enormous for a monarch who with integrity does not believe the Christian faith, or does not believe it in a way compatible with the Church of England.[1]

There is then the issue of morals. The Prince of Wales is one who has acknowledged he cheated on his wife, and has apparently cohabited off and on with his mistress ever since—a sequence which has outlasted the divorce of each of them. His articulated concern for renewed spirituality is not, it seems, to impinge on this area of his private life; and his private life is not as the private life of Edward VII, or of the last Prince of Wales before him—for it is irreversibly public. In the words of his much-loved Book of Common Prayer his extra-marital behaviour has been *'open and notorious'*. If the Ten Commandments were to be read at his coronation (which was admittedly not done in previous rites this century, but is required in ordinary usage of his beloved BCP text) then the anomaly would shriek.

It is easy to recognize that the Prince is in a double difficulty here. If he is unwilling to be celibate and unwilling to distance himself from his mistress, then he has either got to marry her or to continue an extra-marital liason. Both of these courses are fraught with unforeseeable consequences for his popularity and for his constitutional position also. To marry first of all requires the monarch's consent, and that may or may not be available. If it is, it then requires a place and rite for the marriage, and that may be difficult to achieve in a significant Church of England building like the Abbey or St.Paul's.[2] It might have, like the Princess Royal's second marriage, to be done in Scotland, but that would look highly evasive.[3] If it is done, then a status for his new consort in the event of his succeeding to the throne would have to be established. That might be 'morganatic', but such an arrangement is quite unprecedented, and has been entirely rejected in the past.[4] If his marriage were not morganatic, then there would be a full-blown Princess of Wales, a Queen-in-waiting. When the succession occurred and the coronation followed, she too would presumably be crowned, and be communicant also. There is clearly a fear that a somewhat tarnished-looking Supreme Governor of the Church of England would emerge from this semi-farcical yet overtly religious and symbolic event.[5]

---

[1] Christian belief is clearly not automatically built in with dynastic succession ('not of the flesh, nor of human will..'), and the absolute requirement upon a monarch does seem close to conversion with a gun at the head, a missionary method usually deplored by the enlightened.

[2] Church marriages on premises other than parish churches are permitted by the Archbishop of Canterbury's 'Special Licence'. Such Licences, however, are never issued to divorcees, a restraint reflecting the general public policy of the Church of England. But see note 5 below.

[3] At the very point of originally going to press, the Archbishop of Canterbury, Dr. George Carey, stated in Australia (on 5 August 1997) that 're-marriage would create a crisis for the church'.

[4] 'Morganatic' is a term usually employed to indicate that a monarch's marriage partner would be a 'commoner' without royal titles or public roles—and without any rights of succession for any children born to the union. It was an arrangement suggested once or twice to Edward VIII re Wallis Simpson, but rejected by the government of the day. The word is connected etymologically to the German word 'morgen', and in its origins apparently denoted a gift given by a husband to a wife on the morning after the first night of a marriage—perhaps through a suggestion that the marriage is now wholly privately acknowledged, but is away from public gaze.

[5] The first version of this note was written in August 1997 and drew attention to the unknown role that the two princes of the next generation—and their mother—would fill. Since her death at the end of August 1997, there has been a growing interest in the country in the future of the princes. It has to be noted, in relation to the discussion on this page, that the Prince of Wales is now a widower, not a divorcee.

(F) THE ROYAL CHOICES

How then is the situation to be resolved? Disestablishment and separation of Church and Crown would obviously give space and freedom for such a new monarch to be inaugurated with integrity on all sides. On the other hand, it would be quite improper for the Prince's marital situation to be the *reason* for seeking disestablishment—that would almost trivialize a momentous constitutional move, and would suspend the future of the Church of England and its life and government upon an historically contingent individual figure and his inclinations. It would be doubly absurd if the present monarch then outlived him or he himself stepped aside from the succession. On the other hand the issue is too big and would take too long to solve for it to be delayed until he himself succeeds and is immediately facing the issue of the coronation. Clearly, therefore, there is only one way in which the release of Prince and Church from each other can be secured before the crisis comes at that unpredictable moment of succession. It is for those who seek disestablishment *for its own sake* to press now for the cutting of the connection, and in so doing they will incidentally release the Prince.

The initiative for such disconnecting should arise from within the Church of England and its Synod. If it comes from the Palace, it will quite unhelpfully centre on the person of the Prince. If it comes from Parliament, it runs the risk of cutting the Church of England off without our true participation in the decision, and with the possibility of the terms of the cutting loose being arbitrary and unfair. It ought to come from within the Church of England as we seek to be free of that targetted Parliamentary rule which currently still binds us.

But if the Church of England could be disestablished before the Prince inherits, then he and the Privy Council would have great freedom in planning his inaugural ceremonies. This is not the scenario envisaged above, and the content of such an event is too open at the moment for any serious speculation or advice-giving to be undertaken. It would presumably be possible to locate the ceremony in any place around London, or even in a series of places. The Dean of Westminster might (depending upon the terms of disestablishment) still be inhabiting a 'Royal Peculiar', and could allow a Royal national and international inauguration with any proportion of Christian content or none. Equally the Dean and Chapter could probably lend the Chair to other sites if a less Christian ambience were desired, but conservative voices were calling for the tradition of the Chair (and perhaps some of the other ceremonies) to be continued.

I would judge that a dynastic monarch, not now compelled by external forces towards an internal Christian faith-commitment which has to display such visible practice as to be above general criticism, might well have a viable role as Head of State of the United Kingdom and the Britannic Majesty's other territories and domains. It would be an honest and realistic situation. It would leave the inheriting monarch free to express his own religious faith in whatever personal way he wished; and it would leave the rest of us able to recognize good qualities in him as an experienced quasi-politician, without having to worry about whether he spoke or lived or modelled Christian discipleship for the Church of England and its life today.

THE GROUP FOR RENEWAL OF WORSHIP (GROW)

This group, originally founded in 1961, has for over twenty-five years taken responsibility for the Grove Books publications on liturgy and worship. Its membership and broad aims reflect a highly reforming, pastoral and missionary interest in worship. Beginning with a youthful evangelical Anglican membership in the early 1970s, the Group has not only probed adventurously into the future of Anglican worship, but has also with growing sureness of touch taken its place in promoting weighty scholarship. Thus the list of 'Grove Liturgical Studies' shows how, over a twelve-year period, the quarterly Studies added steadily to the material available to students of patristic, reformation and modern scholarly issues in liturgy. In 1986 the Group was approached by the Alcuin Club Committee with a view to publishing the new series of Joint Liturgical Studies, and this series is, at the time of writing, in its eleventh year of publication, sustaining the programme with three Studies each year.

Between the old Grove Liturgical Studies and the new Joint Liturgical Studies there is a large provision of both English language texts and other theological works on the patristic era. A detailed consolidated list is available from the publishers.

Since the early 1970s the Group has had Colin Buchanan as chairman and Trevor Lloyd as vice-chairman.

THE ALCUIN CLUB

The Alcuin Club exists to promote the study of Christian liturgy in general, and in particular the liturgies of the Anglican Communion. Since its foundation in 1897 it has published over 130 books and pamphlets. Members of the Club receive some publications of the current year free and others at a reduced rate.

Information concerning the annual subscription, applications for membership and lists of publications is obtainable from the Treasurer, The Revd. T. R. Barker, 11 Abbey Street, Chester CH1 2JF. (Tel. 01244 347811, Fax. 01244 347823).

The Alcuin Club has a three-year arrangement with the Liturgical Press, Collegeville, whereby the old tradition of an annual Alcuin Club major scholarly study has been restored. The first title under this arrangement was published in early 1993: Alastair McGregor, *Fire and Light: The Symbolism of Fire and Light in the Holy Week Services*. The second was Martin Dudley, *The Collect in Anglican Liturgy*; the third is Gordon Jeanes, *The Day has Come! Easter and Baptism in Zeno of Verona*.

The Joint Liturgical Studies were reduced to three per annum from 1992, and the Alcuin Club subscription now includes the annual publication (as above) and the three Joint Liturgical Studies (with an extra in 1994). The full list of Joint Liturgical Studies is printed overleaf. All titles but nos. 4 and 16 are in print.

Alcuin/GROW Joint Liturgical Studies

All cost £3.95 (US $8) in 1997

1987 TITLES

1. (LS 49) **Daily and Weekly Worship—from Jewish to Christian**
   by Roger Beckwith, Warden of Latimer House, Oxford
2. (LS 50) **The Canons of Hippolytus** edited by Paul Bradshaw, Professor of Liturgics, University of Notre Dame.
3. (LS 51) **Modern Anglican Ordination Rites** edited by Colin Buchanan, then Bishop of Aston
4. (LS 52) **Models of Liturgical Theology** by James Empereur, of the Jesuit School of Theology, Berkeley

1988 TITLES

5. (LS 53) **A Kingdom of Priests: Liturgical Formation of the Laity: The Brixen Essays**
   edited by Thomas Talley, Professor of Liturgics, General Theological Seminary, New York
6. (LS 54) **The Bishop in Liturgy: an Anglican Study** edited by Colin Buchanan, then Bishop of Aston
7. (LS 55) **Inculturation: the Eucharist in Africa** by Phillip Tovey
8. (LS 56) **Essays in Early Eastern Initiation** edited by Paul Bradshaw,

1989 TITLES

9. (LS 57) **The Liturgy of the Church in Jerusalem** by John Baldovin
10. (LS 58) **Adult Initiation** edited by Donald Withey
11. (LS 59) **'The Missing Oblation': The Contents of the earlyAntiochene Anaphota** by John Fenwick
12. (LS 60) **Calvin and Bullinger on the Lord's Supper** by Paul Rorem

1990 TITLES

13-14 (LS 61) **The Liturgical Portions of the Apostolic Constitutions: A Text for Students**
   edited by W. Jardine Grisbrooke (This double-size volume costs double price (i.e. £7.90 in 1997))
15 (LS 62) **Liturgical Inculturation in the Anglican Communion** edited by David Holeton
16. (LS 63) **Cremation Today and Tomorrow** by Douglas Davies, University of Nottingham

1991 TITLES

17. (LS 64) **The Preaching Service—The Glory of the Methodists**
   by Adrian Burdon, Methodist Minister in Rochdale
18. (LS 65) **Irenaeus of Lyon on Baptism and Eucharist**
   edited with Introduction, Translation and Commentary by David Power, Washington D.C.
19. (LS 66) **Testamentum Domini** edited by Grant Sperry-White, Department of Theology, Notre Dame
20. (LS 67) **The Origins of the Roman Rite** Edited by Gordon Jeanes, then Lecturer in Liturgy, University of Durham

1992 TITLES

21. **The Anglican Eucharist in New Zealand 1814-1989** by Bosco Peters, Christchurch, New Zealand
22-23 **Foundations of Christian Music: The Music of Pre-Constantinian Christianity**
   by Edward Foley, Capuchin Franciscan, Chicago (second double-sized volume at £7.90 in 1997)

1993 TITLES

24. **Liturgical Presidency** by Paul James
25. **The Sacramentary of Sarapion of Thmuis: A Text for Students**
   edited by Ric Lennard-Barrett, West Australia
26. **Communion Outside the Eucharist** by Phillip Tovey, Banbury, Oxon

1994 TITLES

27. **Revising the Eucharist: Groundwork for the Anglican Communion** edited by David Holeton
28. **Anglican Liturgical Inculturation in Africa** edited by David Gitari, Bishop of Kirinyaga, Kenya
29-30. **On Baptismal Fonts: Ancient and Modern**
   by Anita Stauffer, Lutheran World Federation, Geneva (Double-sized volume at £7.90)

1995 TITLES

31. **The Comparative Liturgy of Anton Baumstark** by Fritz West
32. **Worship and Evangelism in Pre-Christendom** by Alan Kreider
33. **Liturgy in Early Christian Egypt** by Maxwell E. Johnson

1996 TITLES

34. **Welcoming the Baptized** by Timothy Turner
35. **Daily Prayer in the Reformed Tradition: An Initial Survey** by Diane Karay Tripp
36. **The Ritual Kiss in Early Christian Worship** by Edward Phillips

1997 TITLES

37. **'After the Primitive Christians': The Eighteenth-century Anglican Eucharist in its Architectural
   Setting** by Peter Doll
38. **Coronations Past, Present and Future** edited by Paul Bradshaw
39. **Anglican Orders and Ordinations** edited by David Holeton (December 1997)